I0156441

The Financial Industry's

Guide to:

THE NO BLAMING ZONE

What others are saying about

The No Blaming Zone...

"Enter Dr. Farber's No Blaming Zone and embark on an inspirational journey from Blaming to Empowerment!"
-Jon Gordon, Bestselling Author of The Energy Bus and The No Complaining Rule.

"Blaming others for what you've done, what you're doing, and where you're going hurts you personally and professionally, and it hurts everyone in your life. Dr. Neil Farber's engaging story makes shifting away from the Blame Game possible. Read this book and transform your life now!"
-David J. Pollay, International best-selling author of *The Law of the Garbage Truck: How to Respond to People who Dump on You, and How to stop Dumping on Others*

This story contains a powerful and beautifully delivered message: Take responsibility of your thoughts, attitudes, and actions and you'll be surprised by the growing fulfillment and happiness that follows. It's a quick read that has lasting impact!"
-Dr. Peter Bandettini, PhD. Chief, Section on Functional Imaging Methods, Director, Functional MRI Core Facility, National Institute of Mental Health

"The "No Blaming Zone" is a delightful and entertaining read full of sage advice, numerous useful techniques and references for anyone interested in being happy. In the midst of challenging times and turbulent moments this text helps reaffirm the power of personal ownership of our thoughts and state of being. Far beyond a "self-help" book, I would more appropriately classify it as a "world-help" book. The simple lessons provide a path for further exploration into positive psychology and more importantly how anyone can be a catalyst to make a difference in the lives of others while enriching their own. This will be a must read for all the caregivers on my team."

-Mark S. Gridley, Vice President of Physician Affairs, FHN Healthcare

"...a wonderful book and very easy and quick to read. The concepts are so simple and could make such a difference in a person's life. I would highly recommend that everyone in this world read this and "stop blaming others for their own situation." What a key takeaway! I would highly recommend this book to anyone wanting to improve their outlook on life."

-Denise Augustin, Executive Director, Surgicenter of Greater Milwaukee

"This delightful parable illustrates in a very lively way how to put into action and reap the positive results of making lemonade out of lemons. Carl is a symbol of bad attitude and his enlightenment is an allegory that teaches lessons that all of us can follow. It is a quick read and makes you feel absolutely positive about the power you have over your life."

-Anita Stangl, President & Chief Executive Officer, Alliance for Smiles -- Medical Missions for Children

"The NBZ is a must read for anyone from leadership to the front lines who wants to make a difference in their organization and better understand how environment and attitudes create perceptions that influence our realities."

-Dr. Joseph Kerschner, Dean and Executive Vice President, Medical College of Wisconsin, Professor, Department of Otolaryngology and Communication Sciences Medical College of Wisconsin

The Financial Industry's
Guide to:
THE NO BLAMING ZONE

An allegorically true story about creating positive changes, harnessing energy and achieving potential through the simple act of taking responsibility.

The Financial Industry's
Guide to:
THE NO BLAMING ZONE

An allegorically true story about creating positive changes, harnessing energy and achieving potential through the simple act of taking responsibility.

Neil E. Farber, M.D., Ph.D.

DYNAMIC PUBLISHING GROUP

MEQUON, WI

Other books by Dr. Farber

The Blame Game: The Complete Guide to Blaming: How to Play and How to Quit. Bascom Hill Publishing, MN, 2010.

Making Lemonade: 101 Recipes to Convert Negatives into Positives. Dynamic Publishing Group, WI, 2012.

The No Blaming Zone: Dynamic Publishing Group, WI, 2013.

- Check out Dr. Farber's **Blame Game** blog on PsychologyToday.com

- Like: **facebook.com/TheActionBoard**

- Check out **TheKeytoAchieve.com** to help establish and achieve your goals and your potential best you.

- Contact: TheKeytoAchieve@gmail.com

ISBN - 978-0-9853024-1-2

LCCN - 2012934684

Printed in the United States of America

Contents

Dedication

To my daughter Shoshana (Josiana) Robyn, I dedicate this book. Shoshana lives a life of Positive Power and responsibility. She is full of life, love, compassion and a true altruistic spirit. Shoshana approaches each day with a sense of adventure. She is one of those people who you look at enviously and wonder why she is always so happy. She has never ordered the same ice cream twice at Baskin-Robbins – every day is a new experience. Shoshana guides others out of the darkness by the brightness of her inner light. I love you!

Acknowledgements

Kaelah, Shoshana, and Sarena; my amazing children, you have all contributed in some positive way to this book. I know that you will continue on your positive path to flourishing. You are each succeeding in developing and using your unique strengths in productive as well as altruistic ways.

It's not just my kids who contributed to this book. My parents, Linda and Michael (OBM) also deserve a Thank You for teaching me to appreciate and strive for the positive throughout my life. The lessons that you taught me have been invaluable.

I want to acknowledge and thank my positivity gurus: Drs. Stephen Covey (OBM–you are dearly missed), Tal Ben-Shahar, Ellen Langer, Martin Seligman, Chris Peterson (OBM–you touched many lives), Mihaly Csikszentmihalyi, Barbara Fredrickson, Ed Diener, Sonja Lyubomirsky, Dan Gilbert, and Deepak Chopra.

A special Thank You to two friends, literary and positivity mentors and wonderful authors, Jon Gordon and David Pollay. Mr. Gordon, who has been called the "Pastor of Positivity", has written several workplace positivity books including; *The Energy Bus*, *The No Complaining Rule*, *Soup*, *Training Camp* and *The Shark And The Goldfish*. When I was in search of a mechanism to deliver a message and write a book, he suggested that I tell a story. His insight and inspirations were instrumental to the development of this book. David Pollay, from the first time that I met you I was inspired by your stories and your accomplishments. As you promised, your new book *The Law of the Garbage Truck* delivered a life-inspiring message that hopefully will be translated into every language to be read and implemented by all – thank you.

I have been the lucky recipient of support, knowledge and spiritual inspiration from the following Rabbis, Marc Berkson, Dovid, Menachem, and Moshe Rapoport, Mordechai Spalter, David Cooper, Laurence Kushner, and Joseph Telushkin, as well as The Dalai Lama and Thich Naht Hanh.

Heartfelt gratitude is due to the members and leaders of the Committee on Occupational Health and the Wellness Task Force of the American Society of Anesthesiology as well as the Positive Health Division of the International Positive Psychology Association. With special thanks to Drs. Gail Randel, Afton Hassett, Robert Holzman, and Mary Ann Vann.

To my martial arts mentors who have taught me so much more about life and what it is to thrive than simply martial arts; you are my LIFE coaches, not just my martial arts instructors: Grandmasters John Pellegrini, Avi Nardia, Miki Erez, Moti Horenstein, Dennis Hannover, Chaim Peer, Chaim Bachar, Moni Isaac, and Park Sang Young and Masters Mark Gridley, David Rivas, Paul Chay, and Greg Chay. To my martial arts students, I have learned as much from you as I hope you have learned from me.

Who else to thank? All my surgeon, nurse, anesthesiology, technician, administrators, transport, custodial and secretarial colleagues in the hospital. To the hospital custodians and patient transporters, you are fabulous and, as you know, I couldn't have written this book without you and we couldn't take great care of our patients without you!

Dr. John Kampine, Dr. David Warltier and Dr. George Hoffman – my anesthesiology gurus who have supported and encouraged my rather non-traditional pathway in medicine – you help me bring positive psychology into our practice and our hospitals. Thank You!!

A special thank you to a special person, Rhonda Devorkin. Without your encouragement and wisdom this book would not have been published.

I would like to thank my friends, clients, students, and patients. I am so appreciative that you allow me into your lives. I have learned so much from all of you.

WHY THIS BOOK?

There are several people who are widely acknowledged to be leading experts in the field of positive psychology. These psychologists and authors have each written excellent scholarly books on happiness, optimism and positivity. I have not. I have, however studied most (if not all) of their books and research investigations. I have also studied personality in university and received a Bachelor of Science degree with Honors in psychology. I have studied and performed medical and psychological research in neuroanatomy (the structure of the brain), neurophysiology (how the brain works), biopsychology (how the brain influences behavior), and neuropharmacology (how chemicals affect the brain and how the brain affects chemicals). After obtaining a Doctorate degree in Pharmacology and Toxicology, I completed my medical degree and a research fellowship for a year in neuroanesthesiology – focusing on how various brain areas function and respond to chemicals and medications.

Over many years, I have had the pleasure of teaching a variety of subjects to undergraduate and graduate students, medical students, physicians, and nurses. In addition to scientific topics, I have taught such things as bioethics, conflict management, mysticism, meditation, and a course on wellness for physicians. I have done research on conflict, mindfulness and positivity and established a program to create a positive perioperative environment in our hospital. "Perioperative" refers to what goes on prior to, during and after surgeries. It is through this positive perioperative program that this book found its way out of my brain and onto paper.

I have had the pleasure of interacting with so many people at the hospital who some term *ancillary*. These are people who give generously of their time to transport patients in the hospital and clean the hospital. They are far from ancillary and have a bigger role in patient care than many of us acknowledge or appreciate. Similarly, in every industry there are the shakers and movers who are considered essential to survival of a company and there are the "little people" who are viewed by many as less important. The reality is that everyone and every role are important. It would take less than a week of a custodial or secretarial strike to bring a thriving company to a screeching halt. These are often tedious positions requiring great mental and sometimes physical fortitude. This tale is about one such individual, the realization of his true value, and his importance to the corporation.

While this story is based on real-life situations in a real financial institution, all people in this book are fictitious and any resemblance to real figures is purely coincidental. Enlightened custodial workers and tellers may be found in every bank in every city.

I hope that you appreciate that the positivity and responsibility lessons in this book are not limited to banks or for that matter, even to businesses. They are principles necessary to stop blaming, take control of your life and set you on the road to success and satisfaction in all of your relationships, family, career, and life. Similarly, custodians and tellers are representative of all workers in all industries who are often underappreciated, yet are integral pieces of the puzzle and play a critical role in the smooth operation of any business or corporation.

My life has been like everyone else's life. There are no blessed lives and no cursed lives. Life is what we make of it. Like you, I have had my ups and downs. I have had good days and bad days. As I get older, the number of good days increases. I don't think this is a factor of age, but rather a growing appreciation of the benefits of optimism and positivity and an improvement in my personal techniques for how to cultivate these personality traits. I am not doing this alone. After reading everything that I can find on the subjects of positivity, happiness, and optimism from leading experts in the field, I have analyzed, summarized and consolidated what I consider the most important factors in creating a positive life.

I am very pleased to acknowledge the growing community of businesses around the country who have undertaken the journey of creating a positive workplace environment through the process of taking personal responsibility. These organizations; such as US Bank, DigiCopy Centers, the Functional Magnetic Imaging Center at the National Institute of Mental Health, Children's Hospital of Wisconsin, The Surgicenter of Greater Milwaukee, FHN Healthcare Network in Illinois and Sharp Grossmont Hospital in California have instituted *No Blaming Zone* programs.

The *No Blaming Zone* lessons in this book are not simply academic. Yes, they have been shown to work in scientific studies to improve well-being, success, and satisfaction. But they won't work for you unless you actively apply them to your work, your relationships, and your life.

1. Carl's Plight

Carl parked his car in the bank parking lot and swore under his breath about another day doing something he didn't want to do. He had already started his countdown for the number of hours left until he could get back in his car at the end of the day to go home. Home – that's a laugh! It was an apartment that didn't feel anything like home. For two months now he hadn't been living at home. Home was where his wife Nancy lived with their two kids, David and Cindy.

Carl woke up this morning like he did everyday for the past month, stayed in bed through a fourth round of hit the mole with his snooze button and then slowly made his way to the bathroom.

Another sleepless night and another headache this morning. He looked at himself in the mirror and didn't like what he saw. Carl thought about calling his kids to say, "Hello" since he hadn't spoken with them in a few days and their last conversation was more yelling than talking. He wanted to apologize, but he knew that his wife would prevent him from speaking with them.

Carl and Nancy were separated. Nancy was going to follow through with her promise and file for divorce if he didn't "turn his life around". That was easy for her to say. It was her fault that he was in this position to begin with. She was the one who hadn't supported him when he wanted to be a musician. Life would have been different if that had happened. Life would have been better! More money, more fame, more respect from his kids, more happiness, and he would still be living in his own home…

Carl got out of his car and slowly made his way up the steps into the bank. He gave a shallow nod of acknowledgement to the security officer sitting in the corner who responded with what seemed to Carl like a dismissive hand wave. He looked up at the clock and then glanced down at his watch to confirm that it was now 8:35am and he was missing the "morning huddle". He didn't really understand why he was expected to attend the huddle anyway. It was usually directed toward the sales force and had nothing to do with the tellers. Why should he care what the loan officers were going to do with their day?

Never in his wildest dreams would he have imagined that he would have ended up here. A bank teller; accept deposits, cash checks, and smile even when you don't feel like it.

After high school, Carl was all set for a career as a musician. He thought that college was a waste of time; taking a bunch of classes that he wouldn't really need. So he left university and decided to start working in a music store to jumpstart his career – he would teach on the side and make a lot of important connections. "How could his parents have let him do that?" he would later ruminate. They should have known that he was in no position to make that decision and they should have been more forceful about convincing him to stay in college.

His career in that music store? What a laugh! He should have been promoted to manager after working there for six long years. The owner kept promising advancement but he never came through. Carl worked his butt off for that place and it never paid off. It never paid much; that was for sure.

If the owner had only given him the manager position, his life would have been better. He just knew it would have been better because it would have meant more money, and lack of money was the beginning of the problems with his marriage.

Nancy was a dental assistant who worked hard and made a decent living. Carl and Nancy met when they were in the late teens and he had high hopes and aspirations. She loved his music and encouraged him to pursue his dreams; or so she said at the time. But two kids later and with increased frustration and conflicts at the music store, Nancy convinced him to quit and find a better job. He should never have listened to her. It was Nancy's way of trying to control every part of his life. It was his last connection to the music industry and he traded that in for this illustrious career as a bank teller. "I am truly a loser", he said under his breath.

To top it off, the bank was starting to cut down some of his hours because he had only been there for a short time. They claim that they didn't have enough money. Well, what did they think he had? Did they think that he could afford to work less? It wasn't his fault that he didn't have the seniority. He worked hard. Harder than some of the more senior tellers. Heck, even the senior tellers have almost no authority; they report to the Teller Supervisor.

He started as a teller downtown and after only 2 months, he was transferred to another branch. This new branch was no better than the first one. It wasn't the bank per se; it was the people and the job. They were all losers; people that couldn't get any other kind of work. He didn't mind leaving the first branch and hoped that it would be better somewhere else – but no luck.

Wasn't it ironic? Carl was upset about not working enough at a job that he hated. The sad part was that he needed this job. He wanted to get his life in order but it seemed like someone or something was always putting up obstacles. Someone up there didn't want him to succeed. "Why do you have it in for me?" he asked, looking up at the ceiling with arms outspread.

Harry McClain, the Branch Manager stopped mid-sentence as Carl quietly walked into the conference room and took a seat near the door. All eyes turned toward Carl who turned his palms skyward and mouthed the words, "What?"

Harry continued his morning sermon about balancing efficiency and customer service. He concluded by reminding the sales team that their goal this week was to complete fifteen proactive phone calls.

"See," Carl said to himself, "this meeting was not intended for me."

It was now 8:45 am and Carl knew that meant he only had fifteen minutes to get his workstation prepared, money counted, and his window open. Not opening your teller window at 9:00 am was an unforgiveable sin; worse than showing up late for the huddle. Harry stood and waved his arm toward the door, indicating that the huddle was over and it was time to go to work. Carl was the first to exit the room and headed straight for his window in the foyer of the bank.

"Oh great!" Carl said in a sarcastic tone when he arrived at the window. There were already people lined up outside the door waiting to get in. He noticed some kids outside running around their parents and reflected on how much he missed his own kids.

Ever since he moved out of the house, he visited with David and Cindy every Saturday and Monday for a few hours. His apartment was too small for them to stay over and their relationship was so shaky and stressed, that he was sure that they wouldn't want to spend the night even if they had the opportunity. When his kids were young everything was great. They thought he was the best dad in the world. Well, he was the best dad in the world. He took them to movies and even to the circus. He would do anything for them. But all that had changed. David was now fifteen years old and in high school. He thought he knew everything and when Carl moved out of the house, David thought that he was now the king of the castle. He talked back to Carl and accused Carl of walking out on the family. When Carl told David that he was the one who was asked to leave, David didn't buy it and blamed his dad for the family falling apart.

"Why doesn't David realize that none of this is my fault?" Carl asked of the custodians one day as they passed each other in the hallway. The custodian provided a timely shrug, a friendly smile and continued on down the hall.

And then there was Cindy. Beautiful Cindy. She was his pride and joy. Now at age thirteen, she had already gotten in with a bad group of kids and had followed her brother's lead about how to treat dad. She was the one that he was most worried about, but she was the one least likely to listen to anything that he said. She wouldn't even come to the phone to talk to him. Carl knew that his wife was ultimately the one to blame for his kids' attitudes. Nancy had turned his kids away from him.

If only he had a better job and more money, life would be so different. So much happier; just like it used to be. His relationships with his wife and kids would be perfect again. "If only…"

2. The Boss

"If only what?" asked Harry McClain.

McClain had been the Branch Manager for four years. His rise from teller to personal banker to mortgage representative and then manager all at this same local branch was known to all employees. They were reminded of this at many of the morning huddles when he would talk about motivation and personal goals.

Harry was a distinguished looking man in his late 50's. As the Branch Manager, he wasn't tolerant of anything other than hard work, dedication and a commitment to customer service.

Harry continued, "Why are you always talking to yourself? You know I've gotten complaints from customers about your attitude. They say that you're gloomy and put a negative spin on things. The economy is tough enough to handle without also having to deal with your pessimistic influence."

"Hey," Carl replied quickly. "If you're talking about Mr. Lipstein the other day, he was the one who started talking about all of his problems. All I did was add my two cents worth."

"Ya, he told me that you went into some detail about how awful life can be. How little control we can have over our lives when things like diseases, financial hardships, and *divorce* are knocking at your door. You didn't really talk to him about getting divorced did you?"

Carl didn't answer.

With a look that hovered between exasperated and frustrated, Harry said, "Okay. That's it Carl. Come to my office at your next break."

Twenty-five minutes later, Carl was going on his break. He'd been dreading this break since Harry walked away from his teller window. He gently knocked on Harry's closed door and was told to come in.

Before he could get out a "Hello," he was greeted with, "Close the door and sit down, Carl."

Harry continued, "I've had it. You've got to do something about your attitude or you can forget about continuing your job here. This has happened too many times before and I don't see things changing. We are who we are. Take me for instance. In general, I'm a pretty optimistic person. Take you for another instance. You're a pretty pessimistic person. I think that these things are ingrained deep inside. You are who you are. You can try – but I don't think you can ever really change your basic personality traits. It's like trying to change your height or your eye color. Just like a leopard, you can't change your spots and become a tiger. You just can't do it".

"So then what do you want from me?" asked Carl as he raised both shoulders in an exaggerated shrug.

Harry quietly responded, "What I want is for you to change your behavior. I don't expect that you can be an upbeat, happy person, but I do expect that you can keep your business and your opinions to yourself and stop upsetting our customers! I don't know how else to get the point across to you. You are the face of this bank!"

So many thoughts were swimming around in Carl's head. Why? he thought. It's not my personality. It's my situation. Anyone who had been through what I've been through and what I'm going through would feel exactly the same way. It has nothing to do with genetics. I'm in a tough spot and I wouldn't be normal if I wasn't stressed out and depressed about my life. I'm in an unimportant job, making no money, and I'm losing my wife and my kids. Should I go out and celebrate? The face of this bank? I'm a glorified cashier, he thought to himself.

"Carl, I'm not sure if you realize that I have several responsibilities in this position as branch manager. Only one of them involves trying to get you to provide great service to our customers. I have to make sure that the daily operation of the bank is efficient; that includes operations, lending, product sales, customer service, and security and safety.

Those are just some of the things that take up my time. So taking up my time with these types of motivational talks is not in my best interest. Especially since I don't think it will help you in the long run."

"Look Carl, I feel for you, I really do. But I can't keep you on here working like this when you are depressing your customers," declared Harry.

"Depressing my customers? These people just need to make a deposit or cash a check. This is not rocket science. It's not up to me whether or not they keep coming here. They're more concerned with the interest rates and mortgage rates that we charge. I hardly matter in all of that."

Carl continued, "Mr. McClain, ever since I passed that teller assessment test and got my week of teller training, I've been doing my job and putting in my time."

"I would like you to put in more than just your time. But be that as it may, here's your next assignment. Find a new behavior and a new attitude or find a new job!" demanded Harry.

3. The Reaction

Carl did not take the news well. He knew that he may not be the happiest guy in the world but he certainly is not the King of Doom. When he left Harry's office, he was confused. How customers could be complaining about him was surprising. He was the one who should be complaining about *them*. Who was it? He thought to himself.

Was it Mrs. Davidson or Schneider's teenage daughter? They always ended up at his window. "Lucky me," said Carl. He'd listened to Mrs. Davidson discuss problems with her gardener and about how the weather was "not cooperative" on their last Hawaii vacation. Tanya Schneider had the nerve to complain about how her parents wouldn't give her the car that she wanted for her birthday, and instead she ended up with her dad's 2010 Jaguar XJ something. Carl had lengthy conversations with both of them about being born under a bad star and how rotten luck just seemed to follow some people. Carl wasn't alone in his beliefs about Murphy's Law and being cursed. Both customers were active and willing participants in the conversations.

After just a few minutes, Carl's confusion changed to frustration as he realized how little control he had over these things. The frustration also didn't last long as it rather quickly transformed into anger. Why was he singled out? He was the one who was forced to work this stinking job and the one who was not allowed back into his own house! Of course customers are not happy. The economy sucks and they need more money. That's why they're in the bank in the first place. His job was to deposit their money or change their checks into cash. He wasn't hired to be a psychologist and the last time he checked, nobody was paying him to be an entertainer. Heck, that would be fine with him if they wanted him to play his guitar and sing. That would be a much better job anyway! But if that's what the bank wanted, they should go and hire counselors or clowns or musicians. That wasn't his job!

A final wave of bitterness washed over Carl and left in its trail pangs of anxiety.

"Great, what am I going to do now?" he asked himself. He thought, "How am I going to make ends meet? How am I going to pay rent, make my car payments and my pay bills? How am I going to show Nancy that I can make it and change my life around? How will I ever get my kids' respect again if I can't even keep this low-end job?"

Carl's anxiety and anger dissipated…and was replaced by depression. He came to realize that he was truly in trouble and didn't know how to get out of this quick-sand that he called his life. He realized that all of his worst nightmares about his job and his family were about to come true.

He felt sick.

4. Trying to Cope

Carl made a decision. He would really try to be happier at work. He could do a lot of things that people didn't think that he could do. He would surprise everyone and walk in with a big smile. Well, some kind of smile, anyway. He would focus on being happy and it would happen. He could make happiness happen if he worked hard enough at it. It would also help if he could avoid Mrs. Davidson's and Tanya Schneider...and, of course his boss, Harry.

Carl put on a smile as he walked into the bank. He used a lot of pleasantries and friendly salutations as he greeted the security guard and his fellow tellers. He tried to avoid talking about anything personal and vowed not to talk to the customers about their financial ills or about all of his problems. He did really well for quite a long period of time and then near the end of the first day, he lost it.

He sat at his window and looked over to the other two tellers. They each had several customers in line waiting to be served. He tried to wave people over to his window which was open and available, to no avail. Finally, Mr. Peterson broke through one of the other lines and walked up to Carl's window.

Mr. Peterson was a retired salesman who had worked in the kitchen and bath industry. He had been a loyal bank customer for many years and was well known for always starting off his transactions at the window with, "Wow, if you knew what I'm going through today!"

The tellers would privately discuss how they answer Mr. Peterson. They all had the pre-determined responses. Gail would say, "Wow, I bet it's quite something." Jim would respond, "Mr. Peterson, if anyone can deal with it, it's you." Sarah would answer, "I'm so sorry to hear that, anything you want to talk about?"

Carl would typically respond, "Uh huh, how can I help you?"

But not today.

Carl couldn't find it in him to leave it alone. Instead, he looked straight at Mr. Peterson and said, "You think you have problems? You should try to live my life and see how easy that is for you. Just when you think that things couldn't get worse, your boss calls you into his office and tells you to 'cheer up'. How ridiculous is that?"

Mr. Peterson gave several emphatic nods in agreement. Realizing what he was doing, Carl quickly apologized to Mr. Peterson, reached through the window and dragged back the completed deposit slip along with two checks. Carl again apologized to Mr. Peterson, explaining that he hadn't been feeling well all day and thought that he needed to go home early. Mr. Peterson gave him an understanding smile and thanked Carl for his assistance.

After completing Mr. Peterson's transaction, Carl went over to the senior teller and reported that he was ill and needed someone to replace him. He spent the next several hours worrying that Mr. Peterson was going to report him and that would be the end of his job.

What began as a fictitious excuse for Mr. Peterson became a reality for Carl. Over the next several days, Carl began using up some of his sick time. He was having his typical morning headaches but they seemed worse now. He started having stomachaches and needed antacids to relieve his heartburn.

If he was able to make it into work, he would last about half of the day and then start to feel a little ill. He guessed that these physical signs were, in part, a result of his worrying so much that he was going to say or do something at work that would jeopardize his job, but he also knew that he couldn't control acid reflux just by wishing it away. So he lay in bed, feeling sorry for himself and getting more depressed. He even picked up a pack of cigarettes on his way home from the bank. He hadn't smoked cigarettes since the time he began

Neil E. Farber, MD, PhD

dating Nancy. She demanded that he quit and he hadn't taken a puff since. Seems that she was always demanding something from him. He never should have quit smoking in the first place. It was a great way for him to sit and try to relax a bit before work.

5.   An Encounter

"**O**kay, back at work. Let's try it again today. See if I can make it through the whole day. That would be nice for a change." Carl ruminated. He knew that his sick time was quickly running out and that the extra days off that he was taking were not going over well with his boss or with his coworkers who had to pick up the slack. The thought that he was jeopardizing his job even more by using sick days, of course made him feel worse. Carl remembered how upset he got with Jimmy, one of the other tellers, who called in sick for an entire week. He doubted whether Jimmy was really ill or whether he was faking it to get some things done at home. Well, Carl wasn't faking it. He was truly not feeling well enough to be working. Who could blame him for that?

Carl arrived at the bank at 8:30 am and by the time he made it to the conference room, it was 8:35.

"We start at 8:30 sharp!" Harry McClain directed his comment to Carl who was again taking a seat near the door. McClain was discussing the importance of overages. Apparently one of the newer tellers had some extra money yesterday. McClain explained that when you balance your drawer at the end of the day, overages are just as concerning as coming up short.

"As you know, all outages are recorded and sent to be filed at the corporate bank. Having extra money is not a positive mistake. It's a sign of not paying enough attention to detail. More often than not, the discrepancy is due to careless typing or simple math errors. In other words, human error and you are the human! Corporate sees the mistake and it takes time, money, and energy to create a paper trail to figure out how it happened. So over or short, it doesn't matter, mistakes are mistakes."

McClain continued, looking briefly in the direction of Janice Stanley, one of the tellers who had just completed her training, "Everyone who has been a teller, knows what it is like to be way out of balance, it happens to all of us during our first couple of months, luckily an associate caught the miscounting error...again and so it was not sent to corporate. But this shouldn't happen. Human error is preventable error. Please be more careful, starting today."

A few hours later, Carl was taking his first break of the day and went to grab some coffee in the break room.

"You should have seen the traffic this morning. There was an accident on the freeway. Why don't they realize that being late isn't my fault?" Carl asked of the custodian who was passing by the room at the time.

The custodian repeated his smile and shrug, but this time quietly added, "Nobody should blame you; it's not like you are responsible for your decisions."

"What's that?" asked Carl.

The custodian looked back at Carl and replied, "Oh, I was just remarking that sometimes we give up control of our lives and don't take responsibility for our decisions. We feel a little better by blaming others and this makes us more accepting of our failures and lack of success."

"Oh, excuse me Mr. Psychoanalyst. As if you know anything about my life. You don't know me, or what I've been going through. I will have you know that I am not responsible for all the bad crap that comes my way. There are things beyond my control and I seem to attract the bottom of the barrel when it comes to luck."

The custodian put down his broom, turned to Carl and said, "Do you find that these techniques work well for you?"

"What techniques? What are you talking about?" responded Carl with a frustrated tone.

The custodian replied, "I'm talking about the way that you play the blame game and focus on negatives. It happens to be the opposite approach to the one that works for me, so I was wondering if you're having much success with it."

Carl quickly retorted, "That sounds like a sarcastic and obnoxious remark to me. Look who's trying to give me advice on success; a janitor, the one guy in this bank with a job worse than mine. That's a laugh!"

The custodian replied with a kind smile, a shoulder shrug and then continued his walk down the corridor.

Carl returned to his station, rather frustrated with the encounter. That wasn't the break that he needed from work. That was even more upsetting than work was. From his window, Carl could see the janitor walking toward some plants with a watering can.

One child, waiting in line with her parents for a teller, suddenly ran off toward the custodian and he gave her a high five when she reached him. He gave her the watering can and she proceeded to water the plants with him. After a few minutes, he walked over to the teller line and started a conversation with the child's parents. By now the line had moved forward and Carl could catch a few words from the conversation.

"Well, we really appreciate your help. That was going above and beyond," the mother was saying. The custodian gave that same shrug accompanied by a soft smile, a slight, gentle bow and "My sincerest pleasure." As he walked away, the little girl gave a wave as she returned to her parents' hands and they approached Carl's window.

"Frank is a great guy", said the father to Carl, aiming his head in the direction that the custodian had just walked away. "How did you manage to get him?"

"Just lucky I guess," replied Carl with a dry, unenthusiastic tone. "How can I help you today..."

At lunch, Carl passed by Frank, who was straightening up the magazines around the coffee table.

"One of your clients?" Carl asked jokingly. "Not *my* client. Just a nice kid and her family who I believed could use some thought redirection," replied Frank.

"Thought redirection, that's pretty pompous of you, isn't it? Are you a psychiatrist or a janitor?"

With a broad smile, Frank replied, "I never claim to be a doctor. I'm just a guy who has a great life and I want to help others find the same thing."

With a look of surprise, Carl said, "Has a great life. YOU'RE A JANITOR! You are stuck at the bottom of the food chain, my friend. You are not what I would call a success. Looking at you even makes me feel a little better."

"That's what I like to hear, Carl," said Frank. "That you're feeling better. But I didn't do that for you. You did that for yourself. I've been hoping that you would start feeling better after recently being sick so often."

Carl took a step backward and stated, "How did you know my name? What do you mean, sick so often? I've never even met you before."

Frank put his open hands up toward Carl as if he were gesturing to slow down a fast moving car, "Well, we actually have seen each other several times at morning huddles and so I've heard your name before. But even if I hadn't it would be pretty easy to read your name at your window when you're here. As for the sick time, you hear lots of stuff around the bank if you're mindful…and I try to always be mindful."

Carl responded with a sneer and commented, "It's hard to be mindful when you're doing such a mindless job like we both have."

"Oh my friend, I beg to differ. Our jobs are only mindless if we choose to make them that way. I wouldn't have been able to last long at this career if I didn't do it mindfully."

"Nice try," said Carl "but you're stuck in a dead end job just like I am. You wouldn't be here if you had other choices."

After lunch Carl returned to his station and signaled with a wave to the next person waiting in line. While he was processing the savings account deposit transaction, the customer turned to his left and yelled out, "Hey Frank, do you have a second?"

Carl looked over to see Frank changing a light bulb in the common area. Frank walked over, reached out and shook hands with the customer.

"Hello Jack how's the family", inquired Frank.

"Everyone's great. I just wanted to let you know that I took your advice, went with my gut and things worked out better than I thought they would. That's what brings me in here today, finally making a deposit instead of a withdrawal."

"Well, that certainly is great news. You deserve it," said Frank.

"I feel like I do deserve it and wouldn't have gone through with it without your encouragement. So, thank you," replied the customer.

Frank gave a big smile, "My pleasure, you always had the ability, you just forgot that," he answered, then turned around and walked back to where he was working.

Still smiling, the customer turned back toward Carl, who said, "Frank is an asset to this bank. Do you know that he teaches meditation and relaxation as a hobby? That's what got me tuned back into my career and able to make important decisions. You guys are lucky to have him, don't you think?"

"Sure," replied Carl in a rather curt fashion with a tentative nod, and then added, "Now would you like to get a balance on that account?"

6. A Rose is a Rose

Carl finished the day out at the bank and was not in the greatest mood when he left. He kept thinking about Frank, the janitor, and how Frank had insinuated that Carl was always negative. The truth was that he wasn't always negative. When good things happened, he was at the top of his game and he was a positive person. It just so happened that the past few years had more bad stuff than good stuff happening. It wasn't his fault. He was working as hard as he could, trying to keep it all together and improve his situation. Who could blame him for that?

Obviously Frank made assumptions about him without giving him the benefit of the doubt or fully understanding his current situation. Who was this janitor anyway that he thought he could start treating customers as if he were some psycho-specialist?

Carl backed out of his parking spot at the bank and directed his car onto the street adjacent to the parking garage. As he merged with the oncoming traffic, his mind was wandering back to the day's conversations and interactions with the janitor. What did he have to do with those customers? Why were they so enchanted by him? Why…

"Damn!" remarked Carl, as he bumped into the car ahead of him. "Why did you stop so suddenly," Carl yelled at the driver as he got out of his car. Carl knew that he didn't even notice the car that he hit. His mind was elsewhere and he wasn't paying enough attention.

"You were the one who hit me," replied a rather large man in his late 30's. After both men looked thoroughly over the vehicles and were not able to find any significant damage from the slow moving collision, they agreed to exchange names and phone numbers, but not call the police.

Carl was thankful that he didn't have to report anything because he couldn't afford another insurance hike. That would have done him in financially. "Well, forty good minutes wasted with this mess. If that guy had been more careful and slowed down more gradually, I wouldn't have hit him. He didn't have to jam on his brakes. They ought to take drivers like that off the road," Carl said aloud to no one.

Carl decided to go out to a local tavern for a beer to calm down after the accident. After draining the first beer rather quickly, Carl was determined to savor the next one and take his time to relax.

It was now seven pm. Carl's cell phone lit up and began making chirping noises. "Oh no, it's Nancy. I was supposed to pick up the kids for dinner at six o'clock. Damn it!"

"Hi, Nance, I'm on my way." Carl said as he answered the phone. Nancy replied, "Don't bother Carl, I'm giving the kids dinner here. They didn't want to wait for you again and they were hungry. They have school tomorrow and it's just better that they not be out late. Maybe we can try this again next week."

"Next week? I can't wait until next week! I haven't seen them at all this week," pleaded Carl. "And they haven't seen me. It's important," he continued.

"If it's that important," Nancy asked, "why are you always late or don't show up at all?"

"Oh come on Nancy, I'm not *always* late and when I am, it's not my fault! I would have been on time today, but I had a lot of stuff going on in the bank because of this weird janitor and on my way home I got into a car accident. That's right, a car accident! It's the truth. The guy in front of me jammed on his brakes without any warning and made me hit him. Thank God everyone was alright. I needed to burn off some steam after that and I came over to grab a quick beer and lost track of time. So I didn't do this on purpose. It wasn't like I planned to have an accident," Carl finished.

Nancy let out a sigh and responded, "That's right Carl. Nothing ever was, is, or will be your fault. There's always someone else to blame for your actions. Don't you realize that you play some role in your life and that life just doesn't happen to you? This is the biggest problem in our marriage. You have to take some responsibility for your decisions and actions and until you do, we are never going to get back together again and your kids aren't going to respect you. Whenever things aren't perfect in your life, the first words out of your mouth are, 'it's not my fault'. Well, if you blame everyone for all of the bad stuff in your life, are you also thanking everyone when anything good happens to you?"

"Anything good happens to me?" Carl continues where Nancy left off, "that's certainly a laugh. What good things have happened to *me* lately?"

"You're right Mr. Gloom, life sucks for you. When will you grow up?" said Nancy as she hung up the phone.

Grow up? Take responsibility? Blaming everyone? Mr. Gloom? Who is she talking about? Carl started reflecting on the conversation and was deeply bothered by it. She sounded just like the janitor. Why the heck is everyone picking on me? It's not my fault...

"Hey bartender," Carl called out, "I think I need one more beer."

7. The Janitor

Carl arrived at work and was a little quieter than usual as he reported in and went to the huddle. He realized that he was starting to analyze everything that he said and how he said it. He was self-conscious about the words he was using and was frequently checking to see if he was acting out of line and saying the very things both Nancy and the janitor accused him of saying. After a very careful morning, Carl decided to spend his lunch break trying to find that janitor, Frank.

After about five minutes, Carl found Frank sitting on the carpeted floor with three children. The children were laughing and giggling as Frank made funny faces.

Frank reached into his pocket, pulled out a balloon, which he proceeded to inflate. While the balloon was partially filled with air, he tied it off and started twisting it and turning it. He asked the children, "What do you think this balloon will turn into?"

While they were guessing different animals, the balloon quickly took the form of a hat that he put on the head of one of the children. He pulled out another balloon, repeated the procedure, twisting each section several times.

Again, he asked the children, "What do you think this balloon will become?"

They started guessing everything from another hat to a dog or a bunny. They watched as his balloon became a funny face that he handed to the second child. A third balloon appeared and he repeated the question, this time they hesitated before answering and the oldest child said, "It's hard to know, you could make it into anything."

After the third balloon became a butterfly, which the youngest child immediately reached out to take, Frank excitedly responded, "Exactly! You three are just like balloons."

"What do you mean we're like balloons?" answered the youngest child. "I'm not red and filled with air."

Frank laughed and responded, "No, you are certainly not red and filled with air. The balloons start out looking all the same; but with some twists and turns, they can become almost anything. You three are just like that. You are full of potential and each of you has the ability to become doctors, lawyers, teachers, bankers, writers, astronauts or anything else that you can imagine."

"You made the balloons change their shape," said one of the children. "That's right replied Frank, and you can decide what you are going to become. You have so much power that you can shape your future."

Frank noticed Carl as he approached closer to the group. Frank made his way to his feet and introduced Carl to the children who acknowledged Carl with a smile and a wave of their hands.

Frank said, "Let's go see if your parents are still busy," He turned to Carl and added, "I was just waiting with them while their parents were with a personal banker."

Frank brought the children back to their parents who were just completing their business and walking out of an office. "Oh thanks for taking care of them Frank," they said as they saw the children walking toward them.

"Don't thank me, this was great fun for me," replied Frank. He turned toward Carl as they continued down the hall. "So, how are you, my friend?" inquired Frank. Carl looked down at his feet and responded, "Well, yesterday I would have said, how should I expect to be, given my circumstances? But today I'm afraid to say anything; especially in front of you."

Frank said, "I'm getting the feeling that the negative - blaming approach may not be working out for you as well as you'd hoped. Have you given any thoughts to leaving the dark side and walking toward the light?"

Carl looked up and gave his own version of the shoulder shrug and replied, "How do you know so much about this stuff? Do you mean to tell me that you're always happy and always positive and nothing bad ever happens to you? Do you honestly believe that if I think negative thoughts they will all come true and my life will be really bad and that if I think positive thoughts, my life will suddenly turn around, there'll be flowers in every hallway, I'll be immensely rich and crowned king of the universe?"

Frank turned to Carl with a broad smile and said, "One step at a time, my friend. Let's sit for a few minutes and enjoy the lunch break."

"You know," Frank confided in Carl, "I wasn't always a janitor." "Oh really," said Carl sarcastically, "This wasn't your first career choice when you finished high school – if you finished high school."

Frank laughed and continued, "Yup, I finished high school. I even finished college and got an MBA degree and believe it or not for a brief while I worked as a personal banker. I left banking and worked in some large corporations in mid-level managerial positions, but was never really satisfied. I always knew that I had it in me to be better than mid-level. I was trying to climb the corporate ladder but couldn't seem to make it past the first few rungs. My attempts at success were always being sabotaged by coworkers or by superiors and so I would move onto other companies looking for something better.

I found out that there wasn't anything better. The problem wasn't with the companies. The issue was with me. I was letting everyone else take control of my life. I didn't take personal responsibility for what I was doing. I had choices that I didn't acknowledge or realize that I really had. After bouncing around from job to job, it started getting harder to find a good job because I was considered a high risk and non-dedicated employee. Nobody wanted to touch me. I was highly qualified, but out of work. My money got tight and my fiancée left me because I was always complaining and blaming everyone for my situation. She was smart and bolted when she realized what I was doing to myself and would probably eventually do to her."

With a look of understanding Carl stated, "So that's how you ended up here."

Frank answered, "Not quite. After much self-reflection and several months of unemployment, I decided that what I was in need of was *happiness*. I know that this sounds frivolous, but I felt that this is what I had really been in search of but was not sure where to find it. I had eliminated the fact that I would be able to find it in a big corporate office. I believed that these were not the kind of people that I was meant to be working with. So I started searching. I did some traveling in Asia - India and Thailand, all in the name of searching for the truth and happiness. Fortunately I did find happiness; unfortunately it was gone as soon as the drugs wore off. I was even worse than when I started. I came back to the United States more depressed and with more people to blame for my situation."

Frank took a long swallow from his water bottle and continued, "When I got back to the states, I decided that the best place to learn about happiness and why I wasn't finding it was to take some psychology classes. I loved studying personality psychology when I was an undergraduate student, so I figured taking some classes might give me the fresh start I needed, and give me a clear understanding of what I had spent a lot of time searching for."

Carl was now more curious than ever, "And…"

Frank continued with a smile and a raise of his eyebrows, "And…I found out all about happiness. I read all kinds of great research papers from the top minds in the happiness and positivity fields. I studied about gratitude research and forgiveness research."

Carl interrupted, "Is there really such a thing as gratitude and forgiveness research?"

"Yup," answered Frank, "they are specialized fields of psychology with some very interesting and important findings. There is a whole branch of psychology called positive psychology which studies the strengths and virtues that help people and communities thrive."

"So," Carl asked, "Since you're working here and not in some positive psychology research center, you obviously didn't find out about happiness there, did you?"

Frank nodded and said, "Well, as a matter of fact, I did find out about happiness. I found out tons of very important information about happiness and even wrote a master's thesis on the subject. I didn't complete my doctorate because I thought it was a waste of time. I learned all I could about happiness but it was all academic. I couldn't figure out where to find it and was more frustrated than ever, watching these so-called experts fight for grant money and job promotions and go home to fight with their kids and spouses and go through divorce just like everyone else. It was like trying to be a Buddhist by studying Buddhism in college. I had the knowledge but couldn't apply any of it. By the time I left graduate school, I was in no better shape than when I started; I was more lost and depressed because it seemed like I was destined to be jobless, friendless and hopeless. I had blamed everyone from my parents to my plumber."

Neil E. Farber, MD, PhD

Carl extended his open hands toward Frank and said, "So, I'm still waiting to find out how you got here."

Frank smiled as he took another sip of water, "When I ran out of money and gave up looking for academic and corporate positions, I didn't have a lot of choices. I figured that I would do this for a little while and then move onto something better, although I didn't know what that would be. That was twelve years ago and I've never looked for another job. I'm a lucky guy to be in this position."

"Lucky guy? There you go again speaking nonsense. You have just given up and settled for less. That's not happiness. That's defeat and pretending to be satisfied. That's not healthy," explained Carl.

Frank started to laugh out loud and replied, "I've definitely not given up. I love my job and have finally realized happiness."

"After all the other things that you've done, you finally found happiness as a janitor?" asked Carl with a strong hint of doubt.

"No, I didn't say that I found happiness. I said I realized happiness. I learned to experience happiness. I found out that happy isn't a place or a noun. Happy is a verb; a process that we experience when we are accountable, living in the now and being mindful."

"That sounds like a lot of philosophic gobble-dee-gook", said Carl and continued, "happy is a verb and not a place. What does that mean?"

Frank explained, "I was always searching for a happy place. For something or someone that could make me happy. What I found out was that the more you try to be happy, the harder it is to actually become happy."

Carl asked, "Is that what mopping the floors taught you?"

Frank laughed again and said, "no, shortly after I started working here. I was cleaning up the floor in the main foyer after someone had vomited and overheard a conversation between a teenage daughter and her parents.

Apparently the family had been in here several times within a few weeks to refinance their home and to try to get a loan for medical expenses. Their daughter had been diagnosed with cancer and was now pretty sick. She had just come from getting chemotherapy and that's why she was vomiting. The medical bills were overwhelming; well they would have been overwhelming for most. This family was different.

The father remarked about how they would "just keep trying to get the loan and if it doesn't happen at this bank, there were others."

'We have a limited amount of energy and I want to spend it wisely and in a positive way. Not waste my energy worrying about things I can't control,' he said. He spoke about how he needed to take responsibility for what was going on. It wasn't the bank's fault, the hospital's fault, or God's fault. He was motivated, resilient and accountable at a time that would have been very natural and easy to blame everything and everybody else. I had never seen anyone so successfully step off the blame train. Suddenly, I had an epiphany and so much of the research that I had learned years ago started to take on a new light and finally make sense to me. Happiness was something that I could access at any time. It was my choice and it would have to start with me being accountable for my life."

"It sounds like when you took responsibility for your life, it took away your drive to succeed," commented Carl.

"Not at all," Frank replied. "I found that being accountable was the first step on the pathway to thriving, in this job and in everything that I do. We have become so entrenched in blame that we become controlled by it. We blame people that we love, people that we hate, and people that we don't even know. We blame to avoid or shift our personal responsibility and when we do that we become victims. Everybody is doing something to us! Once I stopped doing that, I regained control of my life."

And with that, Frank put his hand on Carl's shoulder, gave a slight squeeze and said, "Well, my friend, have a mindful day. Time for me to go clean some windows." Frank walked down the hall and disappeared into a storage room.

8. The Bookstore

Carl finished off the day at work, went home and made himself a TV dinner. After dinner, he went out for a drive and passed by a large bookstore. Not typically one for reading books, he was surprised that he had an urge to peruse; and decided to go in and look around.

After a few minutes in the store, Carl found himself in an area that he had never spent time in before; the self-help section. He was taken aback by what he saw; so many books about happiness and positivity. How was he supposed to know which positivity guru, if any, to listen to? He picked up a book called *Happiness,* by Ed Diener and Robert Biswas-Diener and read through the first chapter where it described the importance of "psychological wealth".

Psychological wealth, it said, is how much you are worth in terms of your attitudes, values, spirituality, relationships, health, and activities in which you're engaged. He had never looked at wealth that way before. The book eluded to the fact that things that he was trying to do in his life; like make more money and get a better job have only small effects on happiness.

This is one person's opinion, he thought. Carl looked at other books called *Happier,* by Tal Ben Shahar and *Positivity,* by Barbara Fredrickson. These books said the same things about material wealth and good jobs not leading to happiness. I'm not stupid, Carl thought to himself. Of course I know that money can't buy happiness. But, in fact he had thought that it would be an important part of helping him crawl out of the hole he is in, and that would make him happy. Maybe that wasn't true either.

"Even if I get all those things that I want, I still won't be happy? How can that be?" He asked the books.

Carl continued to look through the shelves. He found a book that he'd heard about called, *The 7 Habits of Highly Effective People*, by Dr. Stephen Covey. He read that it had been called the most influential self-help book of all time. He opened the book and read about Habit One: *Be Proactive*. The whole chapter was about how we should take more responsibility and stop blaming others. He remembered what Frank told him about responsibility being the first step to happiness. Where to start?

The book described how *proactive people* make choices and take responsibility for their choices. They focus on their Circle of Influence – things that they can do something about like work, children, and health. The book said that *reactive people*, who are more likely to blame others, focus on their

Neil E. Farber, MD, PhD

"Circle of Concern" – things that they can't control like the weather and the national debt.

Carl didn't quite understand why children and work would be included in the Circle of Concern since he would have no more control over those things than he could control the national debt. He wondered whether Dr. Covey would consider him a *proactive* or *reactive* type of person.

The one thing that the book said that made sense to Carl was that we all have the ability to choose our words and what we say to others. Carl had always had problems in both his personal and his work life when it came to filtering what words came out of his mouth. Carl knew that his words had often gotten him into trouble but he had always reasoned that he was never the one that started it. He was only responding to what other people had already said or did.

On the other hand, like the book said, everyone still had a choice about the words that they used. Maybe he didn't always have to speak up…

9. Some Positive Results

Carl went to work and decided to focus on talking to his customers, finding out more about them while saying as little as possible about himself. That was funny. He realized that he never really looked at them as *his* customers before. They had been *bank* customers that he was helping.

At first it was very difficult, not referring to his personal life when a customer would complain about something. However, it soon became easier to do and actually allowed him to forget some of his own issues. By noon, he realized that he had had a great morning; maybe the first great morning that he had ever had at this job.

During his lunch hour he walked over to the break room and found Frank joking with some of the loan officers. Carl told him about his wonderful morning, but then added that it could all have been a coincidence.

"Maybe it had nothing to do with what words I used," said Carl.

Frank replied, "The words that you use are hugely important, not just for the people that hear them, but for the person who speaks them. It all starts with thoughts, feelings, and attitude; they influence your words. Your words sway your behavior and people's responses and reactions to you, and your behavior sets the stage for your future – your destiny."

"Maybe some of that is true but your attitude is your attitude. That's something that can't be changed. Even the big boss, Mr. McClain said that you can't teach a fish to fly. It isn't in my genetic make-up to be positive," he explained to Frank.

Frank responded with a smile and said, "Listen, we all fall into different personality types. We're considered happy, sad, optimistic, pessimistic, introverted, or extroverted. They used to believe that this was just the way we were and there wasn't much we could do about it. We could put on a happy face but we couldn't really change what we felt inside. Well, that's just not true!"

"So you think that a leopard can change its spots?" asked Carl.

It's not just what I *think,*" replied Frank, "research has shown that only about 50% of most personality traits are determined by genetics. In fact, heredity only sets a baseline and gives us a set-point. Just like turning a thermostat to increase the heat in your house, you have the ability to increase your happiness or your optimism and reset your baselines – that's the nurture part of the equation. Harry is a great guy and a wonderful boss but I'm sorry to say that about this issue he is wrong. You can control a lot of your happiness and your optimism. As a matter of fact, genetics may only determine about 25% of how optimistic you are. So the problem is that you get to determine the other 75%."

Carl listened intently as Frank described how he could change his outlook. "What do you mean, *the problem is*," inquired Carl. "That sounds like a good thing."

"Well it is a great thing if you are ready to take responsibility for your life, for your decisions and for your feelings. It's bad news if you want to give up your responsibility and blame other people for your unhappiness. The fact is that you have the control."

"That's what I read in *The 7 Habits of Highly Effective People* book," said Carl, "but you obviously can't control everything in your life or even in your *Circle of Influence*. I have to keep this job. I sure wouldn't be working here if I didn't have to. I also can't control my health or my kids. Come to think of it, I hardly have any control over anything."

"You have much more control over your life than you think that you do. You can't control other peoples' behavior or their responses but you can control everything that you do," answered Frank and added, "You don't *have* to come to work. You *want* to come to work."

"Look we're going to have to differ on this one, buddy, because I can assure you that I don't want to work here, I have to work here. But I do think that it is good news that we can change some of our character."

"You can do far more than change some of your character," responded Frank. "We each have a lot more control over our lives than we ever give ourselves credit for. Remember, I once was where you are now. I thought that I had learned so much about positivity and happiness, but the fact is that I couldn't apply most of what I had learned because I was not taking responsibility for my place in the world. I was playing the Blame Game every chance I got and shifting responsibility to someone or something else. Just like you, I always had some reason or excuse for why I was not happy or why I ended up in a certain job or why my relationships were shaky."

"I realize that you may have had it hard growing up," said Carl, "but you can't compare your life to mine. There are many things that I would have changed in my life if it were just up to me. I would have finished college, I would have moved up to a manager position in the music store, and I would probably be a rich and popular guitarist right now – not working at this place; if it were up to me."

Carl's words trailed off. Frank realized that Carl was not quite ready to look that far inward yet. But he felt that the time would soon come for a more honest self-assessment.

Carl abruptly switched topics, "Last night I was reading about psychological wealth and that money and jobs aren't going to make me happy. So then what are the things that I should look for to make me happy?" asked Carl.

Frank looked impressed. "Reading about psychological wealth? Well you really are motivated to make a positive change."

Frank shook his head and said, "It's not a matter of things to look for. People tend to be reactive. We think of things as falling into *Good* and *Bad* categories. When things happen that we call *bad*, we become unhappy and start to blame others. When things happen that we call *good*, we become happy. But those feelings are brief. Those happy and sad feelings come and go as circumstances change. It's unhealthy. It's easy to feel good when things are going great. We need to develop internal happiness; positivity and optimism that don't depend on what goes on outside of ourselves."

"That sounds like a big challenge," said Carl, "Any tips?"

"Tips? Yah, I've got one hundred and one tips," started Frank, "first we all need to re-evaluate what we call *bad*. Much of what people think as bad actually turns out to be good, but they may not see it that way at the time. As soon as you give it the label '*bad*' then you start looking for who made this happen."

"Can you give me an example?" asked Carl.

"Sure," replied Frank. "You're late getting to the airport and miss the plane. You obviously have a good reason to be mad and believe that this situation is bad. You blame the dog for needing water before you left, your kids for having to get dropped off at the babysitters, your boss for giving you an assignment that kept you working late, the alarm clock for not waking you up on time, the traffic for existing, the city planners for poor design, your car for not getting better gas mileage and thus the need to make a stop at the gas station, the airport designers for a stupid parking plan, and the little old lady in the slow moving car in front of you most of the way to the airport. Everything and everybody gets blamed until you find out later that the plane crashed and you realize it was actually a very lucky thing that you missed it."

Frank continued, "How about if you're required to see a doctor to submit paperwork for your new job? You know that you're healthy and think of this as a waste of time until the doctor diagnosis you with high blood pressure and starts you on life-prolonging treatment. Or what if you unexpectedly got fired from a job and after some self-analysis, self-reflection and discussions with your old boss, you make some changes in your attitude and land a dream job with a better company. When you believe in something greater than yourself, it's easy to believe that things happen for a good reason. It's usually our beliefs, biases and outlooks that make things good or bad, not the thing itself."

Carl thought for a minute before he said, "So you think that it's all in my mind that this was a bad job and actually it could be a blessing in disguise?"

"I couldn't have said it better, Carl. Do what you like and like what you do, my friend. Be mindful. That's how you'll develop flow," stated Frank, as he smiled, pointed to the water rushing by in the stream that they could see through the window, stood up and walked back to the supply room.

Carl reflected on the conversation for a moment and then walked back toward his station. When he turned the corner Carl saw David Simmons, one of the customers that he took care of this morning. David's transaction was a little more complicated than usual and involved calling another branch of their bank.

"Hey, thanks for your help this morning, Carl." David said with a friendly tone.

Carl smiled and said, "I'm surprised you're still here." David explained that when he'd finished the transaction with

Carl, he went in to meet with one of the mortgage guys and found out that he was approved for his new home loan.

"What an excellent day!" David stated confidently. With that he reached out, briefly shook Carl's hand and strolled out the door.

10. Mindful or Mind Full

The next few days at work were what Carl would have called "good," meaning that nothing went wrong. No one got mad at him and he didn't get into trouble. He had been lucky and had taken care of several "nice" customers in a row.

He realized that when he was at the bank working, if he thought about problems that he had outside of work, he tended to focus on and ruminate about those things; they brought his mood down and he always ended up feeling frustrated or depressed. If instead, he just focused on his customers, he actually enjoyed himself and time seemed to fly by more quickly.

It's funny, he used to think it would be the opposite. He didn't like his job and so he thought that the more he let his mind wander while he was working, the less he would have to think about what he was doing and time would go by faster. It didn't really seem to work.

Near the end of another day, Carl looked around to find Frank.

"Hey man, how's it going?" Carl asked.

"Excellent!" responded Frank, "A truly rewarding day. Two of our customers called me today to let me know that they had decided to go into business together. I introduced them a few months ago because they seemed to have a lot of common interests."

"Our customers," repeated Carl, "I'm trying to get used to hearing that. You really do think of yourself as having customers don't you?"

"Well," replied Frank, "I don't just empty trash containers, mop floors, and clean countertops. I do a lot of maintenance like taking care of the plants and the big fish tank in the foyer."

"You do that?" asked Carl.

"Yes, I do", replied Frank. "Those are things that customers notice and they help create a pleasant atmosphere. When I interact with the customers in productive ways, I feel like I help them have a memorably positive banking experience. It also frees up some of the extra time that the tellers or the personal bankers may feel like they should spend with customers. I've heard McClain say that tellers should spend an average of four and a half minutes with each customer and that the average time is actually closer to six minutes. That's a lot of production pressure. So, I feel like I'm doing my part. Anyone who interacts with the customers is the face of the company. What's more important than that?"

He continued, "Financial institutions, like most businesses are about finding a balance between good customer service and meeting the sales objectives, good customer service comes first because sales will follow if they build trust with their clients."

"Well, I'm also having a good day," said Carl. "I have had some interesting customers over the past few days. It was a nice change."

Now Frank was curious, "Why do you think that happened, Carl? Are you sure that it was just the customers or could it have been you?"

"Me?" asked Carl. "I haven't changed."

Frank persisted, "Why do you think that these customers were more interesting than your previous customers? Are you sure that it wasn't something that you were doing that made them more interesting?"

"Well," Carl replied, "I have been trying to have more focus on each client, learn more about them, and to not add my own crap into the conversation."

"It looks like you are starting to practice mindfulness," Frank said.

"Mindfulness," Carl repeated with a smirk, "sounds like more psycho-talk."

Frank acted unaware of the sarcasm and responded, "Mindfulness is where you are completely aware and focused on what's going on inside you and around you. You were paying attention to each customer and they automatically became more interesting and important. That's why mindfulness increases satisfaction. Guess what else mindfulness does?" Frank asked.

"I give up," replied Carl.

Frank started getting more excited as he continued, "Mindfulness decreases blaming! First, satisfaction improves when you're mindful and so if you're happy, no one needs to be blamed. Second, when you pay more attention, you make fewer mistakes and so there are less negative issues to blame anybody for. Third, when you are completely involved in the here and now, you are less likely to make comparisons in your mind with other places or other times. Whenever we make comparisons, we are going to be dissatisfied with something and dissatisfaction is one of the leading causes of blaming."

"So," Carl asked, "you think that by focusing on each customer, I was doing this mindfulness thing and that lead to me comparing less, blaming less, and enjoying more?"

"Well put," answered Frank. "I think that's just what happened. I think you are well on your way to a psychological make-over, and boy do you look better, my friend," complimented Frank.

"I feel better too," replied Carl. "I haven't had a headache or stomach ache in days. That flu virus must have passed."

Frank laughed and exclaimed, "Flu virus, you had no such thing. You were attacked by the negative virus. All those negative feelings and emotions can pack a tremendous punch, physically, emotionally and psychologically. That's not just my feeling about it." Frank said. "There's actually research that shows that practicing mindfulness can make you healthier by giving your immune system a boost."

"Really?" asked Carl.

"Yes," said Frank. "Not only that, Ellen Langer, a professor at Harvard did an amazing study where she put a group of men in their late 70's and early 80's into an environment that was set up to look twenty years earlier. She told them not to just pretend that it was twenty years earlier but to actually believe and live as if it were twenty years earlier. After only about a week, the men had less arthritis, more mental acuity, better posture, more physical strength, and better use of their senses. This wasn't just in their heads either, because people looking at their pictures also thought that these guys looked younger than another group of men who were the same age. Being mindful positively changed their lives. They only had people to thank, no one to blame."

"Sounds too good to be true," replied Carl.

"It is too good and it's also true," said Frank. He continued, "Carl, why don't you come by the house and join me and my wife for dinner and a swim tonight?"

Carl was a little surprised by the invitation but decided that he had nothing better to do that night and the company would be a nice change from eating alone.

He accepted the dinner invitation with a little laugh and added, "Oh and I'll be sure to bring my bathing suit."

11. Making Lemonade

Carl followed the directions to Frank's house and was sure that he was either the victim of a practical joke or that he wrote down the wrong address. He parked in the circular driveway of a huge mansion. This house was truly amazing! Carl walked up to the entryway and knocked on an enormous carved wooden door. Frank opened the door with a smile and said, "Hello friend, glad you could make it."

While Frank escorted Carl into the house, Carl was worrying about getting whiplash as his head quickly turned from one room to another, each impeccably decorated. It was the nicest house he had ever been in. Frank took Carl outside behind the house where he found a perfectly manicured garden, a yard that looked like a golf course and a gorgeous swimming pool.

"Did you bring your swimsuit?" Frank asked.

"Swimsuit," replied Carl, "I thought that you were kidding about having a pool. Is this really your house?"

"Of course this is my house, and here's my wife Sarah," Frank said as he extended his hand to the beautiful, black-haired woman walking out of the house toward them."

"OK," said Carl, "What's up with this house? How did you end up here and why the heck are you still working at the bank when you obviously don't need the money? I have serious doubts that you made it this big by being a janitor. Even skimming off the top doesn't sound that rewarding in your business."

Frank nodded in understanding and began to explain what had happened to him. He reminded Carl about how he was working as a janitor when he had an epiphany; coming to a deeper understanding of the importance of responsibility and accountability. Great things started happening for him.

He was sent some money as part of an inheritance from one of his customers. After putting together a little bit of savings, he invested in another customers' new business that became hugely successful. That client was so grateful for Frank's start-up funds when no one else was willing to take a risk and help that he set Frank up with a real-estate investor who made some wise decisions and the rest, as they say is history.

"So you weren't kidding the other day when you said that *you* had a choice about coming to work," said Carl.

"No, I said that *we* each have choices about whether we show up to work," Frank responded with a grin.

Carl ignored the comment and continued, "Well that explains the house." "Now how do you explain why you're still a janitor?"

Frank described the positive energy that he felt from his interactions with the customers. He assured Carl that he recognized the importance of adequate investment and financial advice and that he was not trying to replace the personal bankers, account managers, or financial planners. However, he also understood that he could help customers overcome inhibitions through the use of positivity.

Frank concluded, "I don't just take care of the bank, I take care of the people in the bank. When I make customers and their families laugh and cheer up, I know that they are psychologically on a positive path. Cleaning the bank is like keeping my life clean. I became successful while I was a janitor. I feel that this is my calling and I have changed the job to match my calling. So I like what I do and I do what I like. It's not just that success makes people happier and more positive, it turns out that happy and positive are two traits that can lead to success."

Frank, Carl, and Sarah sat in the backyard relaxing to music, enjoying the weather, and barbecuing chicken. Carl noticed that whenever Frank or Sarah would refer to each other in a story, it was always with praise and admiration. Sarah told Carl that they had been married for over twenty years and that Frank was still her best friend. Frank returned a soft smile and said that he was also in love with his best friend.

Carl thought about his relationship with Nancy. He would love for them to have that kind of closeness and respect; but she never seemed to respect what he did. Things would have been different if only she treated him like Sarah treated Frank.

They all made their way back into the house for dessert as the temperature started to drop. Sitting down in the living room, Carl noticed all of the pictures on the side tables and fireplace mantle. Frank identified their three children in the pictures, one was in graduate school in biology, one was doing a residency in pediatrics, and one was in school to be an accountant, married with a child of her own. Frank told Carl that every Friday night it was their family tradition to have everyone over for dinner.

"It's great," started Frank, "no matter how busy everyone is now that they're older, they still make every effort to join us. We're very lucky," said Frank, smiling as he hugged Sarah, and lifted her up an inch off the ground.

While enjoying dessert, Carl saw a book with an interesting title sitting on the coffee table, *Making Lemonade*: *101 Recipes for Converting Negatives into Positives* by Dr. Neil Farber.

"Great book," said Frank, as he reached over and slid the book across the table toward Carl. "One hundred and one tips, huh," Carl remarked with a smirk. "Yes, sir, it contains techniques and principles that are easy and practical to help you convert all of your negatives into positives; bad things into good things. You know the old saying 'when life gives you lemons...' When I lose my way and start on a negative path, if I ever feel sorry for myself, feel that something is unfair, or I start traveling down the old blaming path again, I pick up that book." Frank stated firmly as he pointed at the paperback on the table.

Carl was really curious now. He picked up the book and opened it to the index where he saw a very long list of recipes for converting negatives into positives, broken down into staples, appetizers, soups & salads, entrees, and desserts.

The very first recipe was *Take Responsibility: don't play the blame game.* This was starting to become a theme. It seemed that everywhere he turned was something to do with responsibility and blaming. Carl then glanced at some of the other titles which also seemed familiar,

- *Happiness comes from doing*
- *Be open-minded*
- *Realize that only you can choose*
- *Value your marriage*

- *Want what you have*
- *Hang with happy people*
- *Believe in something greater than yourself*
- *Look for blessings in disguise*
- *Replace "have to" with "want to"*
- *Help create your personal job description*

Carl quickly realized that he and Frank had discussed several of these recipes. He also knew that in a very short period of time, using some of these ideas had already started to change his life for the better. He looked over the list again and tried to memorize a few more recipes.

"This looks like a lot of work," Carl remarked.

"It's very little effort once you start on the path," answered Frank. "It's a self-rewarding system. Once you understand how to change negatives into positives, the world becomes a better place. When you stop blaming others and they see you taking more responsibility, they tend to do the same. With everyone being more responsible for their words and actions, people get along better and they become happier as you become happier."

Frank continued, "Your optimism and positivity are contagious; it brings out more open-mindedness, non-judgmental attitudes and faith in others which then leads to more positivity. When it starts happening to you it becomes one giant positive spiral upwards that you won't want to leave. Life becomes more fun and fulfilling."

Carl asked, "Does that mean that you don't have bad days or that there shouldn't be any negativity in your life?"

"No, there are a few benefits of negatives, but as most peoples' lives are so entrenched in negativity, they have a long way to go before there is too little negative. In fact, a psychologist, Barbara Fredrickson, who's famous for her work on positivity…"

"She wrote a book called *Positivity,*" interjected Carl excitedly, "I saw it at the bookstore."

"That's right," responded Frank. "Fredrickson found that you don't need to eliminate all of the negatives, you just need to focus on positivity over negativity."

Frank went on to explain that Martin Seligman, the founder of positive psychology identified that focusing on Positive Emotions, Relationships, Meaning in your life, and Accomplishments – what he calls PERMA, results in flourishing or thriving - succeeding in life, marriage, or business. When negativity rules, the results are floundering – poor marriages, poor teamwork, and poor life performance.

Flourish or flounder – what a choice, Carl thought. He began to understand how important the positivity was but still wasn't quite sure how much of it was his choice versus what others chose for him.

As if listening to his thoughts, Frank said, "You know Carl, the holocaust survivor, Viktor Frankl, who lived through the most gruesome concentration camps said, 'When we are no longer able to change a situation - we are challenged to change ourselves.' He found a way to change himself and still find meaning and purpose in his life. I know that you can too."

The evening was getting late and as Carl was thanking Sarah for her hospitality and conversation, Frank appeared from around the corner and handed Carl the *Making Lemonade* book. "Here you go my friend. Use it well and enjoy it."

"I really appreciate this", Carl replied, "but I can't take your book."

Frank smiled and said, "I'd love to say that I'm giving you my only personal copy, but the truth is that I thought you'd like this book and so I ran out to the store this afternoon and bought you a copy."

With a broad, sincere smile Carl gratefully took the book, tucked it under his arm and walked out to his car.

12. The Epiphany

Carl arrived home and instead of going to bed he opened up the *Making Lemonade* book that Frank had given him. On the inside cover was a handwritten note that read,

If you aren't happy with something or someone, you can always change it. The "it" doesn't necessarily refer to the something or someone. The "it" also refers to your state of mind. Appreciate the amazing amount of control you have to make positive changes in your life. Don't blame others for your situation; thank them for allowing you to have new opportunities to grow.
Your Friend, The Janitor

Carl reflected for a few minutes on what he had just read. Did he really not take his share of responsibility for his decisions? Can he always change "*it*" when he's not happy? Everything that he was learning and practicing lately was taking him to new places. Life was more exciting than he ever remembered it being. He was hopeful and interested. These two emotional states were distant memories from his teenage years, and were resurfacing now in middle age. Not too late for a change, he thought to himself. With that he opened up the book to the introduction.

Carl read about lemons. He was starting to understand that even though this book was about making lemonade, there was more to do when you are given lemons. The book discussed how we think of lemons as intrinsically bad, and as soon as someone suggested that you were given lemons or your car is a lemon, the assumption is that it's a "bad" situation.

On the other hand, the book described the wonderful things that you can do with lemons including: bleaching your clothes, whitening your teeth, and treating scurvy. So lemons aren't bad, it's our biases, thoughts and perceptions that place them in that category. The Making Lemonade book isn't all about making lemonade and trying to find ways to add sugar and manipulate lemons to be tastier; it is also about how to redefine what may initially seem to be badness and how to recognize blessings in disguise. He was now starting to see how you could view lemons as good; useful and beneficial. Funny thing is that ever since he was a kid, he loved to suck on lemons. He never understood why so many people thought they were sour.

Carl read about how to view people and events with open and unassuming eyes. He read about how to reinterpret what may, on the surface be bad, but in reality is beneficial.

The first step in the process of changing *bad* into *good* is to not mindlessly label things that initially make us unhappy as "bad." We should try to assume that there is probably more to every story that we don't know which would redefine the thing or the person or the event that appears to be "bad" as actually "good." Good versus bad is more about perception than about the absolute nature of things. This made sense to Carl, although he knew that it would take some effort, focus and thought redirection to achieve this state of perceiving positives when he initially sees negatives.

Next, Carl read the chapter about embarking on a journey and how failures should be viewed as part of the process to success. If everything happened very easily and effortlessly, then you wouldn't be adequately prepared for challenging situations when you arrived at your destination. Be thankful for challenges.

There are no failures; except if you fail to try. The knowledge that is gained and the sights seen along the way will help you train better, perform better and appreciate more fully in the future. The unsuccessful trials were a great opportunity to broaden our minds and enhance our creativity.

Without challenges, there would be no meaningful successes. Carl had failed enough times that he was now finally starting to understand that these could each be valuable lessons from which he could learn and benefit.

Carl went on to read a recipe called, *Value process over product*. In this chapter, he learned that we shouldn't place all of our focus on the summit. Enjoy the climb. The journey is where we learn resilience, hone our skills, and gain experience. You may climb the mountain and never look up, waiting for the summit. But if you never make it to the summit, you've wasted a lot of time and energy and missed seeing a lot of beauty along the way.

He learned about the history of discovery and invention; how mistakes have significantly contributed to many discoveries, which only occurred because scientists were focused enough on the process, not simply the outcome.

Carl understood that there was a common theme here. If we believed that there are no failures, view challenges as beneficial, and focus on the process, rather than the outcome, we would interpret fewer things as being "bad." If there were less bad things that happened, there would, by default, not be as much stuff to blame on other people.

After his discussions with Frank, Carl realized that he had already started practicing some of these techniques. He learned that mindfulness would change our perception of the world, help us to stop comparing and help us to be healthier psychologically. He was starting to appreciate that every time he would think about how good the past was or could have been, the present didn't seem that great – and he would then look for someone to blame for that.

Carl returned to the first recipe, which was about blaming. Before he started reading, something inside of him made him want to put the book down and go to bed. He didn't understand why he felt that way. He wasn't tired. In fact, he felt remarkably awake and alive. He was really enjoying the book and had gotten a lot out of it so far, so it wasn't boredom. Did he not think that this was going to be a worthwhile recipe? Did he think that this chapter wasn't really going to be anything that he could really use? Carl ignored the urge to put the book away and read the blame section.

After finishing, he understood why he was initially hesitant to read this chapter. It was all about him. He finally began to appreciate how much he relied on blaming and accusing others to relieve himself from responsibilities in his life.

As psychologist and author, David Pollay would put it, Carl was acting like a garbage truck, dumping his garbage on everyone else.

Carl realized that even at Frank's house when he was thinking about Nancy, what he had initially viewed as a positive thought - his wish that he and Nancy would have a better relationship, he now understood that it was actually a negative thought. Not only wasn't he happy or satisfied with his current situation, but he was blaming Nancy for putting him there. That was what Frank had meant by his note in the book.

It was like getting splashed with a bucket of cold water on a hot summer day. It wasn't refreshing; it was a not-so-subtle shock to his system. He closed the book and put it on the table. He laid back on the couch in his living room and closed his eyes.

So many thoughts rushed through his head – he felt dizzy. He thought about his approach to life. He thought about how he had blamed everyone else for where he was today. He remembered accusing his school counselors and his parents for his decisions about school.

He had accused the owner at the music store of making a bad decision in not making him the manager. In hindsight, it was probably a great decision for the music store. He probably wouldn't have made a great manager. He was not exactly someone who would go out of his way to help the company. He had blamed the whole music industry for not making him a success. He had blamed Nancy for the teller job that he took, had blamed his financial troubles for problems in their marriage and blamed Nancy for his relationship problems with their kids. Could it be that all of his life was based on blaming?

It was apparent to Carl that nowhere did he have either feelings or thoughts about his own responsibilities. The funny thing was that Nancy had said this to him many times before. He remembered hearing it from her. In fact, he even remembered hearing the same thing from his parents years earlier.

Carl quickly got up off the couch, walked into his bedroom, looked at his reflection in the dresser mirror and said, "What was Frank saying the other day about having a life-changing epiphany? Well, my friend, you just had yours. Don't let this moment go to waste! No more excuses. No more mindless blaming!"

The next day, Saturday morning, Carl went over to his computer and googled, "The Blame Game." He found a book specifically devoted to *The Blame Game: The Complete Guide to Blaming, How to Play and How to Quit.* Was it coincidence that the Blame Game book was also written by. the same guy who wrote the lemonade book?

He drove to the bookstore, bought the book and then took it with him to a local restaurant. Carl found a comfortable corner booth, ordered a cup of coffee and began to read.

After several hours, a side of hash browns, and a few tall glasses of lemonade, Carl had gotten about half-way through the book. He had so many thoughts floating around in his head about how he had blamed, why he had blamed so many people, and how he was going to use the techniques in the book to take more responsibility and stop pointing fingers.

He felt like starting immediately but wasn't sure exactly where to begin. He knew that he needed a plan and didn't want to let this new knowledge and these feelings slip away. He headed home, wondering how he could be both rejuvenated and exhausted at the same time.

13. Taking Control

Carl showed up early at work Monday morning and took a small piece of paper out of his pocket and re-read a note that he had written to himself.

Don't blame - take control - I can make a change!

He smiled as he thought about what his note meant. How much power he had to change his life? He was starting to realize that if he couldn't change what he or someone else was doing, he could still change how he perceived it, which was still effectively changing his life for the better.

He had spent much of the weekend trying to come up with examples of what he could control in his life and what would be really hard to control, like how he felt about certain things.

He was still smiling as he walked into the morning huddle and took a seat near Mr. McClain. He was actually looking forward to working today to try out this new information and his new attitude. It was like wearing some outfit to work and wanting everyone to notice it.

"Hey everyone, check out my new outlook," he wanted to yell to everyone in the conference room.

It was now mid-week and Carl had been on time for the morning huddle every day. He started appreciating these meetings more and was able to find some bit of value in them. Overall, it was turning out to be a pretty easy week at work.

A few hours into the morning, Carl walked outside behind the bank building to take his break. He loved the outdoors and it seemed that he wasn't spending enough time enjoying it. He leaned against the metal railing and looked out toward the stream and the trees in the distance.

It seemed that Carl was getting the hang of this responsibility thing. He had stopped saying the words "if only," and started appreciating his job more. When he had had an outage error this week he took complete responsibility for it, which both shocked and impressed his supervisor and Harry McClain.

As he recognized that he had more control over his life than he had ever suspected, each day was getting a little easier for Carl to think more about his customers' needs than his own, and he was actually starting to enjoy his work. It was funny, many of the problems that seemed to bother him in the past about his job, seemed to have been resolved.

Was he fooling himself? Was he just pretending not to let these things bother him or did they really not matter anymore because there were more important things to focus on?

Carl stood up and moved away from the railing to find some heavy and deep indentations in his forearm from the railing. He remembered how much the metal seemed to be poking him when he first came outside and then it no longer bothered him. In fact, he completely forgot about the railing while he was deep in thought.

He had experienced this before. At first something pushing on your arm or leg is uncomfortable but after a few minutes you have to look to see if it's even still there because you don't notice it anymore. The pressure hasn't changed. Once you notice it or you move your arm just a little bit, all of a sudden you feel the pressure again. So what changed is either our perception of the pressure or the pressure stopped stimulating receptors as much after sitting there for a little while. Either way, it proved that our bodies can completely ignore something that initially may be bothersome. That was great news! If our bodies can do it then maybe so can our minds.

Carl called his wife during lunch to try to schedule his next time with the kids. Nancy mentioned that Carl sounded good over the phone and asked him if he wanted to take the kids for dinner that night. He was pleasantly surprised that she asked him, and he gladly said, "Yes." He would pick them up for an early dinner and promised to have them home in time for bed.

Late in the afternoon, Carl was at his station and after assisting the last customer in line, Frank appeared at his window. Carl again thanked Frank for the excellent evening at his home and for the gift of the *Lemonade* book. Carl also let Frank know about his epiphany while reading the recipe on blaming, how he found and read some of *The Blame Game* book, and how he was determined to change his life.

As impressed as he was about Carl's strong drive for learning and self-improvement, he couldn't help but laugh upon hearing that Carl had spent the weekend reading *The Blame Game*.

"If I had known that you were going to buy that book, I would have given you my copy of *The Blame Game*. So how are you going to start this process?" asked Frank.

Carl explained his theory about negative things acting like something pushing on your arm and how we quickly become unaware of it.

"That is a great analogy," replied Frank. He continued, "Remember that it is important for you to acknowledge and convert negatives into positives, don't just try to ignore them and hope they go away."

"Yup, that's going to be my big challenge," answered Carl. "And I'm up for the challenge," he stated with his chest out and his chin held high. "I already have a greater appreciation of my job, so it must be working."

Frank was excited. Carl could have said this was going to be a problem, but instead he chose the word challenge.

As Carl was leaving the bank to go home, he heard a voice call out from behind, "Have a good night, Carl." It was Harry McClain.

"It'll be a great night," replied Carl.

"Hey, I've been hearing good things about you lately," said Harry. "Don't know what's gotten into you, but keep it up. Seems like you're in the zone."

"I'm in the No Blaming Zone, sir," answered Carl. "You're in the what?" asked Harry. But it was too late. Carl had already rushed out the door, excited to see his kids.

14. Judge Favorably

Carl's attitude at work had improved, he was certainly complaining less about the job, and had taken more control of his life. As he became more mindful at work and concentrated on the here and now, he was less focused on the past; he felt that there were less bad things happening to him and thus fewer people to blame for anything.

However, despite feeling better in general, Carl still had difficulty with people disappointing him and doing what he considered "stupid things."

On the drive into work, Carl was stopped at a traffic light. Just as the light turned green and he started pulling into the intersection, a car drove right through the yellow light as it was turning red. Carl jammed on his breaks and as the car came to an abrupt stop, Carl's coffee spilled from the holder and all over the front of the car. Carl let out a series of profanities and was still mad at the unknown driver when he entered the bank that morning. Several times during the day, Carl referred to the incident and let everyone know about the "idiot" who was driving and caused the spill.

Toward the middle of the day, Carl was taking a break and came upon Frank. Carl started telling Frank about what had happened that morning.

"Yes, I heard all about how stupid that guy was", Frank interrupted.

"What do you mean that you heard?" asked Carl.

"Well word is all around the bank this morning that you were blaming someone for spilling your coffee," answered Frank.

"This isn't like the other cases of me not taking responsibility," replied Carl. "I was sitting in my car when this guy drove..."

Frank interrupted again, "I know, I get it. But you are still blaming him for what happened and bringing that negativity into work with you. Instead of focusing on how great a day this is or could be, you accuse and focus on something that you interpret as negative, bringing everybody down a negative spiral with you."

"Oh no, you mean I'm doing that again?" asked Carl. "So how would you look at this problem?"

Frank responded, "First, let's not make it a problem. If it's a problem, then we probably have someone else to blame for that. So let's try to look at this as a situation, an issue, a challenge, or perhaps even an opportunity. Do you know that successful Fortune 500 companies don't have any problems? They only have issues, situations, and challenges that they turn into opportunities. That's why they're thriving. The companies who have problems are the ones who spend more time blaming, accusing, and floundering."

Frank continued, "Viewing opportunities as problems is a major cause of blaming. By figuring out how to get off the blame train, we are going to become empowered and start to bring everybody around us into the positive light."

"Okay, I understand that," said Carl. "No problems, only opportunities, so how would you look at this situation?"

"Great question," said Frank. "When someone does something that you initially consider bad, there are four "E's" that we can perform to help us judge them more favorably.

We can try to *Explain* their behavior instead of complaining about it. Try to figure out why they might have done that.

If you can't come up with a great explanation, then make up an *Excuse* for their behavior, rather than assuming that they are bad, inconsiderate people, we can assume that they are reasonable and good. Now why would they have done that?

To help make excuses, we should have *Empathy* for others and really try to feel what they might be feeling when they do that. Imagine you were in their shoes.

In addition to empathy, it's really important to *Externalize* for others."

"Externalize?" asked Carl. "I just started reading about that in *The Blame Game* book. That's where you give people the same reasons that you would give yourself if you did the same thing."

"Exactly," responded Frank. "When we do something *bad* we attribute the behavior to something other than our personality, something external to ourselves – because we believe that if not for that external pressure or influence, we wouldn't have done that bad thing. When someone else does something *bad* we typically attribute their behavior to their personality or disposition – so we internalize for them. Psychologists called this making a fundamental attribution error. So one of the ways that we can stop blaming others is to externalize for them – give them the same reasons that you would have given yourself had you done the same thing...and most likely you have done the same thing!"

"In other words, I should be giving people more of the benefit of the doubt, instead of assuming that they were out to get me or that they are just evil," said Carl. "Does that also mean that I should give an excuse to people who truly do bad things like commit murder?"

"No," replied Frank. "I'm not suggesting that all behavior should be excused. However, your goal is to be happy and not to dwell on things over which you have no control. If it's important enough to bother you, then do something about it. Get out of your car and talk to the person that you are blaming. If you choose not to address the issue, then find a way to let it go. Using the four E's to judge favorably and give the benefit of the doubt is a great way to get over it. Carrying it with you is like walking inside a bubble of negativity. Anyone interacting with you has to join you in your negativity bubble, and put up with your blaming and complaining. Not a very positive and productive basis for a healthy relationship. You'll get commiserating and sympathy but that's not very fulfilling. It'll disrupt your current relationships and inhibit you from making solid new relationships."

"What about when people are responsible for making errors at work. Shouldn't they be blamed for that?" Carl asked.

Frank responded, "No, they shouldn't be blamed, they should be held accountable. It's called causal attribution; it's kind of a politically correct version of blaming. The difference is that in those situations we want to decrease the chance of that error happening again. By not pointing fingers in a damaging way, we can try to recruit the involved person to make positive changes and look for ways to improve the system as well."

Carl took this talk to heart. He finished reading about blessings in disguise and judging favorably in *The Blame Game* book and read similar chapters in *Making Lemonade*. He realized that several times per day he was blaming friends, coworkers, and even complete strangers for all kinds of things. He had been a quick and rather harsh judge. Now he realized that he wasn't just hurting others with these thoughts and feelings, he was also limiting and hurting himself.

Carl was determined to apply the principles of the four E's and would focus on giving people the benefit of the doubt. He found that the more he learned about his coworkers, the easier it was to be empathetic towards them. It was eye opening for Carl when he found out that everyone had issues they were trying to work through at home and they each had things at work that they weren't happy with. A lot of their complaints about work were the same problems he used to complain about. Now many of those issues had disappeared or had become unimportant. People that would never give him the time of day before, now seemed to be seeking him out to talk to him about their lives; both good and bad things.

Carl was finally getting to know some of the other tellers, personal bankers, account managers, mortgage representative, and financial planners at the bank. After two months at the first bank where he started as a teller, he didn't even know the names of many of these people and he didn't care to learn them. Now his coworkers seemed nicer and more personable. He was starting to consider them as friends.

Carl stopped at the store to buy some chocolates for Nancy as a thank you for letting him take the kids for dinner. While he was waiting in a rather long checkout line, he noticed a woman maneuvering her way into the line ahead of him. His initial reaction was to get mad and start blaming her for making him late to get the kids. He could feel his heart start pounding, his fists clenching, and his blood pressure raising. He quickly recognized what he was doing and made up a realistic excuse for why she had entered the line. She was probably late to pick up her own kids who were younger than his kids and had no one there to babysit.

He also understood that he was the one who decided to stop at the store and if he hadn't done that, her actions would not have any influence on him. Immediately he felt better about what was happening. He started to relax and let go of the situation. He felt the stress dissipate and his blood pressure return to normal. He smiled; this was not a problem; this had been a great opportunity to see if he could truly apply the lessons for judging favorably.

15. Turning it Around

Carl drove over to the house and knocked on the door. "You're here early", Nancy said as she opened the door. She gave Carl a smile as he handed her the chocolates and he returned the smile. He couldn't remember the last time that he had seen her happy. She called out to David and Cindy to come to see their father.

The kids slowly walked over to the door to say hello. David reached out to shake hands with Carl, who held David's hand and tried to draw him in for a hug that was met with moderate resistance. Cindy similarly gave her father only a tentative hug and pulled away quickly. They said, "Goodbye," to her mother and they headed for the restaurant.

Dinner went better than he thought that it would. David actually opened up and talked about his friends and his school. He told Carl how well he had been doing on his basketball team and asked him if he would be able to start coming to the games. When Cindy realized that she was being left out, she started getting more involved in the conversation and told her dad about some of the goofy things she did with her friends in and out of school.

This felt like a new experience to Carl. Sure he had spoken to his kids before, but he never remembered hearing all of this news and the excitement in their voices. Of course, he had always loved his kids, but he had never been that interested in some of their stories. They really were growing up and becoming interesting young adults. Carl took David and Cindy home a little early, not wanting to get in trouble with Nancy. As the kids went into the house, Nancy could see that their demeanor and behavior toward their dad had improved.

Instead of a quick goodbye, Nancy surprised Carl by asking, "Would you like to join me for a drink?" Carl thanked her for the invitation, politely refused the drink, but said that he'd love some coffee.

Carl felt a little uncomfortable sitting in the easy chair while Nancy sat by herself on the loveseat and what he was about to say increased his own nervousness.

"I want you to know that I'm truly sorry," said Carl.

"Ok," Nancy replied with a sigh. "What happened now? Did you lose your job? Did you have another problem with the car?"

Carl couldn't control himself and started to laugh. "Lose my job? No way. It's the best job I've had in a long time and I'm very good at it too. I was apologizing for the way that I've been behaving and what I put the family through. I just wanted you to know that I don't blame you for any of it. I'm taking responsibility for all of the bad crap that I did."

"Who are you and what have you done with my husband?" Nancy exclaimed, half-jokingly.

"It's really me," replied Carl. "I've been trying to use everyone and everything as an excuse for my failures. But now I've realized that I can't blame anyone for not having a good job, not being able to relate to my kids, and not having a supportive wife, because I do have all of those things. It just took me a long time to realize that."

Nancy told Carl that she had been waiting a long time to hear him say those words and asked him what inspired the change.

"My job, the people I work with, my clients, and an enlightened janitor." Carl replied.

He told Nancy about some of the customers in the bank that he had been assisting. "It's hard to feel sorry for yourself when you see what they are going through and how so many of them still have a positive attitude and zest for life."

"Wow!" said Nancy. "If this is real, it sounds like you are on the right path to turning things around."

Smiling, Carl said, "Oh this is as real as it gets." Afraid that he might say or do something stupid and not wanting to push his luck, Carl stood up from the chair and told Nancy that he had to get to work early and should be going home.

They gave each other a warm hug as Carl got to the front door. David and Cindy, who were performing a 'spy kids' routine on their parents, saw this and came to the door to say goodbye as well. This time Carl got a nice hug from both of the kids. Carl left the house feeling great – better than great. It was cathartic. He had apologized so many times before that he would even joke with his friends that he should just start and end every day by apologizing to Nancy for things that he did or didn't do. But this was different. This was, as Nancy said, "real." He was sincere and she knew it.

At work, as Carl learned more about his co-workers. He started looking at all of the bank employees, not just the other tellers, as his co-workers. He appreciated that each position in a bank branch had its own personal responsibilities and tasks that make the branch function efficiently as a whole, but that wasn't enough. To provide excellent customer service to the clients, everyone needed to have a general knowledge about all aspects of banking and great working relationships not just with other members of the team but also with members of other teams. This is needed to help with making smooth transitions from one banker to the next.

Carl also became more aware of how many of his customers would benefit from meeting with personal bankers and account managers and was now better equipped to provide specific in-bank referrals. He was not just communicating with bank clients, he was developing productive relationships.

16. Apply the Message

A few more days passed and Carl continued to read and use his *Lemonade* book to make positive changes in his life. *Be flexible. Be open-minded.* He was learning and using these daily, and with every recipe that he would incorporate into his life, he felt a little more empowered and powerful.

Two recipes that Carl took to heart were *laugh* and *create a humor depot.* He started renting funny movies, reading comic strips, and learning some new jokes and funny stories. He would relay these to his customers and soon became known for his jokes and ability to make even the most austere clients laugh. Many clients would specifically request him by name and stand in line for his window when they came into the bank.

Carl starting seeing all of these recipes in terms of becoming more accountable and responsible. For example, being more flexible and open-minded would lead to greater tolerance, less rigidity, and less blaming. Learning to laugh at yourself and finding the humor in a situation would lessen the chance that you'll get upset or mad when something unpleasant occurs, and again, less blaming.

Carl's positive attitude became contagious among his coworkers. At first a few of them were blaming him for manipulating the system to get all of the "good" (happy - pleasant) clients while they were getting the "bad" (unhappy - bitter) ones. When he heard about these rumors he discussed it with those tellers and realized that many of them were at the same place that he was a few months ago.

Frank found Carl in the lunchroom as he was talking to some of the tellers. "Happy is a verb," he told them. "It's a process and you can realize it by doing something that you enjoy. I really like being a teller and finding out about our clients' businesses and what makes them tick. The customers know it and they appreciate it."

Later, when Carl was alone, Frank approached him and said, "Looks like you've jumped off the blame train and you're becoming a psychologically healthy and wealthy man."

Carl smiled and replied, "It's funny that you say that because yesterday, my wife Nancy actually complimented me and we had a great conversation on the phone – first time in a long time for that. It felt great."

After a short period of time Carl was promoted to Teller II and then to Teller III. In this position he was responsible for new accounts, the vault, and safe deposit and branch operations. Teller III's were also expected to provide more leadership and training to less experienced tellers.

Neil E. Farber, MD, PhD

After only one month in this new role, Carl got a message that the branch manager, Mr. McClain, wanted to see him. He showed up at McClain's office and with a friendly wave said, "Good morning Mr. McClain, what can I do for you?"

"I need you to sit down for a few minutes to discuss something important," said Harry. Carl took a seat and Harry continued, "What are you doing?"

"I'm sorry," replied Carl. "What am I doing about what?"

"Well, for the past month all I've heard from customers, tellers, supervisors, personal bankers, and even account managers is about how great Carl is doing at work. So I want to know what's going on?"

"Oh that," Carl said with a grin. "That was just me changing my spots."

Carl proceeded to tell Harry what had transpired and how he found out that life was what you make of it. He was now taking responsibility not just for his actions but also for his thoughts, feelings, responses, and attitudes.

Harry nodded knowingly and said, "Well, I honestly didn't have faith that you could make that change but now that you've done it and taken responsibility for yourself, how would you like to take responsibility for the other tellers in the department?" He continued, I'd like you to take on the job of supervisor for the customer service department."

With a surprised look, Carl quietly said, "Jeez Harry, I wasn't expecting this, I don't know that I'm ready to supervise anyone."

Harry brushed his hand through the air and said, "The other tellers respect you, you seem to have a calling here and I can't think of anyone else that I'd rather have as a supervisor. I'm confident that you can do a great job at this."

Upon hearing this, Carl stood up and with a broad smile, put out his hand and said, "Thanks Harry, I accept the position. I really appreciate your trust in me and you can count on me asking you a lot of questions."

Carl left the office and immediately called his wife. He and Nancy had been speaking more regularly and doing so without any arguments. He had been spending more time with the kids and they seemed to really appreciate the time.

"Nancy, some good news, and I'd like to have dinner tonight to celebrate... Yes, *all* of us."

After dinner, Carl and Nancy let the kids know that they had decided that it was in everyone's best interest if Carl moved back into the house. This news was met with cheers and smiles from David and Cindy.

17. Pass on the Message

A few months after Carl took over the supervisor position, there was a regional meeting where tellers in the district gathered together to share information and updates as well as celebrate the fact that several branches had reached their sales goals for the quarter. This was going to be a rally-type event and Harry McClain asked Carl to give a pep talk at the meeting.

"A talk?" Harry asked. "What would I talk about?"

"That's easy," responded Harry. "How you were able to turn our customer service department around by incorporating those responsibility techniques that you're always talking about. After watching you interact with the other tellers and with our clients, it's obvious that this stuff really works."

Carl agreed and gave a lecture about personal responsibility and how to stop blaming others. He discussed how to give the benefit of the doubt and how to empathize and externalize for others.

His talk was very well received and following the conference Harry asked Carl to add a few words during their branch's morning huddles.

For the next few months, just prior to the end of the morning huddles, Harry would let Carl talk for a couple of minutes about responsibility, mindfulness, or some aspect of positivity.

Carl would have periodic meetings with Harry to discuss how the branch was doing and Harry would give Carl more in-depth details about the inner workings of the bank.

Carl gained a greater appreciation for the Sales Team and their responsibilities. He learned that the loan officer's job involved applying the bank's lending policies in evaluating the risk associated when loaning money to a particular customer. They were responsible for negotiating, underwriting and coordinating the closure. They also had the stressful task of denying a loan application.

As Carl's understanding of the banking industry grew, he realized that whether employees were tellers, selling mortgages, giving financial advice, helping broker loans, or performing maintenance duties, they were all customer service representatives.

Carl also learned more details about Harry's job. As the Branch Manager Harry was expected to develop new deposit and loan business; provides a superior level of customer relations and promote the sales and service culture by coaching, guidance and in general motivating the staff. Harry needed to encourage individual and branch sales goals by developing new business sales and referral. He was also ultimately the one responsible for retaining great relationships with account holders. To add to his regular responsibilities Harry was also taking over duties for the Operations Officer who had been ill and unable to come in to work. Carl could see how hard it would be for Harry to do his job well and not be fully accountable.

As Carl grew to have a greater understanding of the banking industry, he was asked by Harry to share the morning huddles and take on the role of providing a motivational pitch for the sales and the service teams.

After getting the OK from Harry, Carl approached Frank and asked him if he would like to contribute to the morning sessions since he was more of an expert. Frank politely declined and told Carl that he was very satisfied with his position in the bank and that he would be available for any help that Carl might want. Carl used the time at each session to pass on information that he had learned from Frank and from the readings that he had done. He would also use himself as an example of what would happen if you didn't take responsibility.

He'd explain, "I used to have all kinds of physical and emotional aches and pains. I relied on Motrin and Tylenol and even alcohol to ease the pains. I no longer suffer from any pains, haven't needed any medications or alcohol, and haven't even had a cold in several months. Maybe I'm lucky or maybe this stuff really works. I don't want to stop to find out."

Harry McClain was happy. It was obvious that there was a great sense of camaraderie at their branch and it became a wonderful environment in which to work. Harry's branch had consistently high marks for employee satisfaction and sales were at the top for the district branches. As Manager, Harry was responsible for his branch achieving goals by actively participating in sales management programs.

Carl learned that another responsibility of the Branch Manager was to increase and improve visibility of the bank within the community. Carl remembered how many "business friends" Frank had and after Harry's approval, he asked Frank to develop a display table where they would advertise a local business or business person. Frank eagerly accepted the task which allowed him more opportunities to interact with bank customers in a broader sense; Frank considered this maintenance - maintaining the bank's good standing in the community.

After two months, Carl was told that he and Harry were going to meet with the district manager - Harry McClain's boss.

Carl knocked on Harry McClain's door and was asked to come in. Judy Street, the District Manager was seated in the leather chair across from Harry.

"Come on in Carl and have a seat," requested Street.

Carl was both excited and nervous about the meeting and asked, "OK, I give up, do you want me to give another talk?"

"A talk? No. Not a talk. I heard your lecture at the conference and wanted to know what kind of psychology training you have had," inquired Street.

"No formal psychology training," responded Carl. "Just an interest that's turned into a hobby while I was trying to pursue happiness."

"Well, aren't we all in pursuit of happiness?" asked Street.

"That's true," replied Carl, "but I found that the harder you search for it the more elusive it can become. Happiness comes more from doing things that we love than from having things that we thought we wanted. Happiness from external gratification is fleeting, conditional and usually insignificant. But happiness that comes from within is deep-seated, long-lasting and usually really profound."

"So, where did you learn all of this stuff?" She asked again."

"From an enlightened janitor and some great books like, *The No Complaining Rule, The Law of the Garbage Truck* – about how to make changes in a work environment, *The Blame Game: The Complete Guide to Blaming,* and *Making Lemonade*: 101 recipes to change negatives into positives."

Street asked, "Do you have any other ideas along the same lines as the lecture that you gave? I would like to find out what messages you think would help other tellers because we've been talking about incorporating some positive psychology and positive health principles into our company."

Carl thought about the question for a minute and then responded, "Yes. I would like to create a financial *No Blaming Zone* for all of the branches throughout the district."

"A No Blaming Zone? What would that entail?" asked Street.

Carl responded, "I'd give lectures and workshops on how we should each take responsibility for all of our thoughts, feelings, actions, reactions, and attitudes. Letting people know how the path to empowerment, success, and personal growth begins with responsibility. The buck stops here."

Judy Street smiled and said, "I was hoping that you would say something like that Carl because that would fit in well with the new job that I am offering you. I would like you to become a District Supervisor for Customer Service. In this new role, you would be able to go to each branch, assess their needs, give talks and promote your new program."

"So what do you think about spreading some of this accountability around?" asked Judy Street.

"I think the whole banking environment should make these responsibility changes, both for the clients and for the working folks like me. In fact not just banking, but every business and workplace should incorporate these principles to improve their customer and employee satisfaction.

"You could start to develop it in this branch and then take it district wide. Bringing your thoughts to the rest of the banking industry and the entire industrial world may have to get put off for a few weeks..." She gave a broad smile, and finished, "So I gather that's a *yes*."

"That's an *absolutely yes*!" responded Carl.

18. The Afterward

Carl was excited at the prospect of being involved in a *No Blaming Zone* project.

He continued to deliver his message at the morning huddle every day typically revolving around a chapter from the *Lemonade* recipe book. And then once per week he would have a brief get together with the tellers and the sales team at his branch for a motivational session that he would call the *No Blaming Zone*.

At these brief meetings they would go over Neil Farber's, *The Blame Game* book or he would review some positive psychology principles that he learned from Ed Diener's, *Happiness*, Tal Ben Shahar's, *Happier* and *Being Happy*, Daniel Gilbert's, *Stumbling on Happiness*, Sonja Lyubomirsky's, *The How of Happiness*, Jon Gordon's, *No Complaining Rule*, *Soup*, and *The Positive Dog*, Stephen Covey's, *The 7 Habits of Highly Effective People*, David Pollay's, *The Law of the Garbage Truck* as well as several other positivity texts. There were so many great books with positive messages!

Each week Carl's messages became more popular with the employees. His confidence grew, such that he would

Neil E. Farber, MD, PhD

actually be able to take these principles, techniques and strategies to the other banks within the district.

Carl put up a sign in his new office, it read:

NO BLAMING ZONE

Take Responsibility - Stop Blaming

- You are responsible for your thoughts
- You are responsible for your feelings
- You are responsible for your words
- You are responsible for your actions

- You are responsible for your reactions

Bring substantive issues to management, if dealing with them will improve safety, efficiency, or satisfaction.

No mindless blaming allowed!

He scheduled a *No Blaming Zone* Session at the bank branch that he had started working in before transferring to his current branch. He was a different person back then and would have really benefited from hearing these messages himself. But would he have really listened to someone preaching these things to him? What would have made the difference for him in terms of whether or not he would have actually paid attention to these words of wisdom?

He believed that it was his own personal story that might create "buy in" to the program. The tellers at this bank knew him when he was the old Carl. He was hoping that the difference would be apparent and he could explain the reason as *taking responsibility.*

Carl started his first meeting at his old branch, "The first step that I learned in positivity training was to get off the blame train and take responsibility for myself. That doesn't just mean for the things that I do, but for all of my reactions as well. I now believe in accountability. When I was working here, I blamed everyone for my problems and everything was a problem. It wasn't until I became accountable that I was able to start turning my life around and fully realize how lucky I truly was."

Some of the tellers who remembered Carl were resistant and doubtful at first but quickly warmed up to the idea as they realized that the person speaking was not the same person who had been a teller and their coworker at the bank.

After just a few weeks, they were feeling better about their jobs and their clients. It was a healthy education and a great example of a positive energy spiral.

When things went wrong at work, when there were miscounts, or wrong balance outages in the drawer, someone failed to send out transaction papers at the proper time, or neglected to check and record proper identification, employees actually took responsibility and didn't spend time blaming each other or complaining about other people. It was a pleasant change. It allowed the team to perform a root cause analysis – getting to the root of the issue, to improve the process, decrease mistakes and improve efficiency and customer satisfaction.

He brought copies of his *No Blaming Zone* poster, which they proudly displayed, on the bank wall.

After having some success with his old branch, Carl started taking the show on the road, traveling to other branches in the district.

The focus of Carl's lectures was about how to become accountable, how to focus on flexibility, open-mindedness, and how to judge favorably. He had them do exercises to enhance empathy and improve their ability to externalize and explain rather than complain. He taught about how mindfulness would allow them to stop comparing, appreciate the here and now, and not play the blame game.

Carl had another meeting with Judy Street. She informed Carl that she had spoken with some of the branch bank managers where he had started running his *No Blaming Zone* program. She told Carl that the consensus was that there was really a positive difference not just in the employee's attitudes, but also in the customers' attitudes. Clients were coming to the bank in a much better mood.

Street told Carl that when they initially discussed bringing in new motivational programs to improve customer satisfaction, one of the managers suggested that they hire some clowns to hang out in the bank. "The idea of team meetings and morning huddles had never been hugely popular," she explained. But Street recognized that what they were doing was much more important than just making customers smile at a clown.

They discussed how responsibility training led to a positive outlook among employees and more work engagement. Carl explained how people could consider their work either as a job, a career, or a calling. The more they felt that what they were doing was a calling, the more engaged they felt at work and the more fun and empowered they were. As they became more involved in work, employees started coming up with great suggestions as to how to improve efficiency and customer service. Engagement at work resulted in more innovation. Greater employee satisfaction and attitudes translated to greater client satisfaction and attitudes. They were also a lot more fun to be around!

Street arranged for Carl to meet with several branch managers to discuss the benefits of his *No Blaming Zone* project. She explained to Carl that as the District Manager her duties included implementing strategies to reduce overhead. This included decreasing absenteeism and sick leave. Corporate had looked at and analyzed this issue and found that Carl's branch had the lowest sick leave and job turnover in the district. Bottom line: not only did this relate to employees being happier and healthier, this also resulted in lots of money saved by the company.

In addition, Street claimed that she was required to develop and execute a plan to get, retain, and grow small and medium businesses as well as personal relationships. She had been getting a lot of good feedback about Carl's idea for the display table and how that was positively impacting area businesses as well as improving the bank's image to maintain a strong local presence. She was planning on using this same concept throughout the district.

Carl quickly became known as the resident responsibility expert. He was often invited to give presentations at various committee meetings.

Not only was work going well, Carl also continued to make *Lemonade* in his personal life.

He and Nancy were getting along better than ever. They reconnected on many levels and their marriage was not only a top priority but also extremely satisfying. His kids were doing well and were actually starting a positivity club at their school to teach other kids what they had read and learned from their father.

Carl was out with his family for dinner one evening. As they were walking back to the parking lot, they saw the driver of the car in the next parking space open his door and hit the side of Carl's car.

The driver looked up and when he saw Carl approach, lifted both hands up and quickly exclaimed, "It's not my fault! You parked so close to the line, how did you expect me to not hit your car? These parking spaces are so close together it's impossible to not hit the car next to you. And the guy on my other side parked his car so close to the edge of this space that he left me no choice…"

The driver was still going on about who to blame, when Carl started laughing. He turned to Nancy, David and Cindy and repeated, "It's not my fault, sound familiar?"

Soon the four of them were all laughing while the driver of the other car gave a shrug of his shoulders and a perplexed look.

19. Conclusion

Value and respect everyone.

Frank, the custodian in this story and Carl, the bank teller in this story are real. I don't know them as individuals and their characters in this book are fictitious but I know that they do exist somewhere. Throughout the world there are amazing individuals who have found their calling in work that many would consider menial labor or "low-end" jobs. Just as there are no unimportant people, there are no unimportant jobs.

As just two examples, tellers and janitors both play a critical role in delivering high quality banking. Personal bankers cannot operate in isolation. Tellers, account managers, auditors, bank analysts, underwriters, loan review officers, chief compliance officers, risk and portfolio analysts, project analysts, secretaries, foreclosure managers, human resource personnel, internet technologists, branch and district managers, mortgage specialists, machine operators, drivers, janitorial and custodial staff, wealth managers, security personnel, maintenance personnel, internet and computer experts, and many others are just as vital to being able to accommodate customers.

You can't remove rungs of the ladder and still be able to climb to the top. The best bankers in the world can't adequately take care of clients if they don't have the right information, training, or knowledge. Banking, like almost every other business and profession, is a team effort.

We may not think of janitors and maintenance personnel as being part of the banking industry. However, if there were no custodians at our local bank, the bankers would have to take their time to empty trash, change light bulbs, clean windows and countertops, and vacuum, etc. It wouldn't take long before that bank was not a place in which you would feel fine about spending time in addition to the fact that the waiting times would be excessive if the bankers were also performing maintenance activities.

This story isn't about banking reform. It's about individual mind reform to develop more personal responsibility and more personal initiative in everything and every job that we do. These characteristics will lead to more innovation, creativity, resilience, engagement and positivity at work. While these thoughts, feelings, attitudes and behaviors will positively affect every business. Individuals alone cannot do it all.

For organizations to succeed they need to also adopt positive organizational behaviors and attitudes; encouraging innovation, personal initiatives, creating opportunities for advancement – not just for money and promotion but also in terms of education and responsibilities. Autonomy needs to be subjectively appreciated by employees, not just given word service by the management. Employees want to know that they share similar community and social values with the company and that the company values and respects them as individuals. Organizations can also enhance engagement by encouraging friendships among employees, enhancing worker creativity, and focusing on establishing strong managerial connections with their employees.

Everyone involved in production, manufacturing, distribution, and management is critically important to the health, well-being and optimum functioning of any business.

Thus, in addition to mutual respect and appreciation for everyone's role in the process, each individual must also acknowledge and accept responsibility for themselves, stop blaming others for their condition and start on the path to satisfaction, health, and well-being.

We are guaranteed the right to the pursuit of happiness and many of us spend a lot of time looking for it. Happiness is elusive. Satisfaction in business and with life often evades us. We give up responsibility and blame others when we don't think we are on the right path and instead waste our time asking, "Why me?"

Neil E. Farber, MD, PhD

Sometimes what we are looking for is right in front of us but we may not appreciate what we have. When you respect and value others, you will be open to hints, suggestions, guidance and words of wisdom from everyone. You could wither away while waiting for Buddha or the Messiah for guidance.

Appreciate that words from an enlightened janitor may be more meaningful than advice from a frustrated clergyman. The responsibility to listen and make positive changes in your life is up to you.

Quitting the Blame Game

✓ Take responsibility

✓ Acknowledge that you have control

✓ Be mindful – focus on the present, no comparing

✓ Redefine bad

✓ Realize that failures are steps to success

✓ Change problems into situations, challenges and opportunities

✓ Believe in something greater than yourself

✓ Give the benefit of the doubt

✓ Judge favorably

✓ Explain – don't complain

✓ Excuse

✓ Empathize

✓ Externalize

✓ Make Lemonade

QUICK ORDER FORM: The No Blaming Zone

Email orders: TheKeytoAchieve.com

Please send the following books. I understand that I may return any of them for a full refund – for any reason.

☐ The Blame Game

☐ Making Lemonade

☐ The No Blaming Zone

☐ The Financial Industry's Guide to the No Blaming Zone

Please send more free information on:

☐ Other Literature ☐ Speaking/Seminars ☐ Consulting

Name: _____

Address: _____

City:_____ State: _____Zip:_____Telephone: _____

Email address: _____

Sales tax: Please add 5.7% for products shipped to Wisconsin addresses.

Shipping by air:

U.S. $4.00 for first book or disk and $2.00 for each additional product.

International: $9.00 for first book or disk, $5.00 for each additional product.

About the Author

Neil Farber received his Bachelor of Science degree with Honors in Psychology at Arizona State University and went on to complete doctorates in Pharmacology and Toxicology and a Medical Degree from the Medical College of Wisconsin. Dr. Farber has been inducted into Phi Beta Kappa and Alpha Omega Alpha Honor Societies. He has received numerous research and fellowship awards, is a practicing Pediatric Anesthesiologist, an Associate Professor of Pediatrics, Pharmacology & Toxicology and Anesthesiology, and certified life coach. He regularly lectures on positivity, wellness, mindfulness, and conflict management. Dr. Farber is a regular contributor for *Psychology Today's* Happiness section, is a high-ranking Martial Arts Master and enjoys spending time with his family. He is the founder of The Action Board© – the next generation in goal-setting tools. Dr. Farber is involved in international medical missions in South America, Israel, Asia, Africa and the Philippines to which a portion of the book proceeds are donated.

Contact: TheKeytoAchieve@gmail.com

Like us on Facebook: www.facebook.com/TheActionBoard

www.ingramcontent.com/pod-product-compliance
Lightning Source LLC
Chambersburg PA
CBHW051728090426
42738CB00010B/2154